Henry Moore

Will Grohmann

# THE ART OF
# Henry Moore

**Harry N. Abrams, Inc., New York**

LIBRARY OF CONGRESS CATALOG CARD NUMBER 60-7798

# CONTENTS

## LIST OF ILLUSTRATIONS

The measurements given refer to height unless otherwise stated. l. = length.

Today Henry Moore's fame and stature are established facts. He is the first British artist since the great painters of the 18th century to win international acclaim and to achieve a leading role among his contemporaries. Within his own country he has inspired the younger sculptors and has encouraged them to follow a line of development that, despite its debt to him, is as independent as was his own. Henry Moore has not only initiated a new tradition but has also become the teacher of British artists.

The author has received much enlightenment regarding the nature of sculpture and much stimulation from him for which he is deeply indebted. He also wishes to express his gratitude for the ready assistance in supplying photographs and information. Further thanks are due to the Marlborough Fine Arts Gallery, London, and the Knoedler Gallery, New York, who, as the sculptor's representatives, graciously helped the author.

## MEETING WITH HENRY MOORE

"If one is to talk about one's contemporaries at all," says T. S. Eliot in an essay on poetry, but which applies equally to the other arts, "it is important to make up our minds as to what we can affirm with confidence, and as to what must be a matter of doubting conjecture. The last thing, certainly, that we are likely to know about them is their 'greatness', or their relative distinction or triviality in relation to the standard of 'greatness'. For in greatness are involved moral and social relations, relations which can only be perceived from a remoter perspective, and which may be said even to be created in the process of history: we cannot tell, in advance, what any poetry is going to do, how it will operate upon later generations. But the genuineness of poetry is something which we have some warrant for believing that a small number, but only a small number, of contemporary readers can recognise."

It is, then, the genuineness of a work that has a direct effect in its own time, and it seems to be this genuineness that is meant when we speak loosely of greatness. We rarely do speak of greatness, for who would dare to judge the moral or social significance of even a recognized sculptor or painter. In discussing personalities of the 20th century, we usually refer to the great precursors or teachers, and we come with a considerable degree of unanimity upon the same names. There are not many of them: of the painters Matisse, Picasso, Kandinsky, Klee and Mondrian, only Picasso is still alive; of the sculptors Maillol, Brancusi, Gonzalez, Picasso, Laurens and Arp, only Picasso and Arp are still active. Through their achievements they have become examples to the next generation, especially to those who were and remained independent and saw in these artists more than merely their achievement. A painter like Klee or a sculptor like Brancusi has almost become a legend. People want to know who these men were. How they lived and what they did, said and wrote, is of interest because of the light it throws upon the historical situation as a whole. The words "moral" or "social" frequently crop up in the judgment passed upon them by their contemporaries. Gropius once said of Klee that he was "the highest moral authority at the Bauhaus", and this judgment is confirmed by his students. Historical greatness begins with the creation of a myth, but only rarely does this start during an artist's lifetime.

The following generation, those artists born in the 1890s, among them the sculptor Henry Moore, are also discussed and, though with restraint, evaluated. It is true that their work has been in the foreground of the thoughts of artists and art lovers for a whole generation, but its connexion with the immediate present through exhibitions, commissions and honours is so acute that no myth has yet had time to form.

Henry Moore occupies a special position among the leading artists of his generation, in so far as he is the most influential of the sculptors. His work exercises a striking influence in every country in the world, even in Japan, and yet Moore is anything but a genius of adventure, like Picasso. Whereas the latter keeps the world on tenterhooks by his Protean metamorphoses, Moore, quite to the contrary, has a great capacity for persistence. Not that he does not change, but his strength lies in the continuity of his creative powers and their gradual intensification. The Reclining Figure that first emerged in 1929 still preoccupies him today; he chose this figure as the theme for the 1957 UNESCO monument and some fifty versions of it exist: no two of them are exactly alike, yet they are all related to one another. The theme of the Mother and Child has preoccupied him since 1922, the outset of his career, and it is still not exhausted. Other themes emerge and disappear again and yet all are intermingled, as though in Henry Moore everything springs from one and the same basic source, which determines his activities as a sculptor and as a personality.

He radiates calm; the first impression one receives on meeting him is that of a tranquil man, who goes his way unperturbed by current trends, events or successes. He is reserved and modest; he has a high, intelligent forehead, lively, inward-looking eyes, an expressive mouth. He lives as unobtrusively at Much Hadham, a village 30 miles north of London, as Maillol at Banyuls or Klee in Bern. He works almost incessantly, travels only when it is unavoidable, and steers clear to the best of his ability of invitations, juries and meetings. He is a trustee of the Tate and National Gallery and a member of many commissions, nor can he always avoid important congresses, but he prefers to remain at his farmhouse with the big lawn at the back and the two studios that contain only the barest necessities. There is no luxury anywhere. He receives his guests with the ease of a man who owes his freedom to his work. Art is to him the natural outcome of an activity in which the hands are as important as intelligence and intuition. Everything in him has developed in a dogged struggle with his tasks; his ideas spring from professional activity, not from speculation; he thinks as he works, and writes the same way. The horrified amazement his sculptures at first aroused forced him to occasional explanations, but these never went beyond the framework his own visual experience. A gay and kind man with sound commonsense, Henry Moore is relaxed in a way that carries conviction; he approaches his work with a discipline that borders on the superhuman. After any enforced interruption, he is able to take up his work where he left off as though nothing had happened; he can retain the impetus for a project until its final realization. The fiery temperament of a Picasso is alien to him; his genius lies in vigour and consistency and in the intensity with which

12

he increases his demands on himself. When we see the small, wiry man working among large blocks of stone and tree trunks, it is hard to understand how he can have accomplished so much. Constant activity would not have been enough; mental energy and an iron will that enable him to realize his visions on even the largest scale, and a perseverance that permits him to work every day alone explain the volume of his output and the extent of his influence.

# YOUTH AND EDUCATION

Henry Moore, like the herald of his fame, Sir Herbert Read, comes from Yorkshire, a hard and intelligent landscape. Castleford, south-east of Leeds, where he was born on 30 July 1898, is a town of 25,000 inhabitants, with coalmining and a glass and chemical industry. He attended the local elementary school, at the age of twelve obtained a free place in the secondary school and received support from the art teacher, Miss Alice Gostick, who sensed his talent and encouraged his interest in medieval sculpture. At eighteen he became a teacher in his old elementary school, while also drawing assiduously, modelling and absorbing everything he came across in the way of art. This was not much, and there were no art books, for the school library was small. At home his interest in art was regarded with misgiving.

His father, Raymond Spencer Moore, had been a miner and had worked his way up to a higher position by intelligence, self-education and industry; his mother Mary was completely taken up with her domestic tasks; Henry was the seventh child and money was short. There had been no artist in the family before him, or any other exceptional personality. His father's greatgrandfather had immigrated from Ireland, and perhaps Moore's Irish-Celtic streak explains the predilection for the early and inchoate in Irish-Anglo-Saxon art; perhaps there the 'Upright forms' of later years echo the tall Irish crosses that often rose to a height of 30 feet, and were decorated with scenes from the Bible. Even the slightest Irish element frequently acts as a powerful ferment in the spiritual life of England.

In February 1917 Moore joined the 15th London Regiment, was gassed during the battle of Cambrai (November 1917), sent back to London and demobilized in February 1919. He first became a teacher, but in September 1919 he received an ex-service grant which permitted him to study at the Leeds School of Art for two years. It was a school of the old-fashioned type, and Moore has little to say about this period except that he spent a whole year drawing from models and plaster casts and that none of his teachers had anything to give him. The city of Leeds could scarcely compensate him for the shortcomings of the Art School; nevertheless, it was a city of half a million inhabitants and it has a Town Hall "in the Palladian style", a few churches, St John's dating from the beginning of the 17th century and St Peter's which possesses old tomb slabs and a Saxon cross, and in its immediate vicinity stood an abbey in the late Romanesque style. This was more than Castleford had to offer, and at twenty-two Moore must have been looking for fresh stimuli.

In any case, we know that in Leeds he came into possession of a book by Roger Fry, 'Vision and Design'. It caused him great excitement, for it was quite different from such writing on art as he had previously come across; for example, what he had read about

Michelangelo when he was seventeen. From Fry's book he learnt for the first time of Negro art and Mexican sculpture, and was confronted by ideas on completely three-dimensional sculpture and truth to material. Negro sculpture, he read, is more essentially sculptural than its European counterpart, more so even than medieval European sculpture; its forms are completely three-dimensional, whereas with us the final goal is representation, and by the time our sculpture reaches its culmination it is "generally already decadent from the point of view imaginative significance". In Negro sculpture the neck and torso are cylinders, the heads pear-shaped, the faces concave, the limbs scarcely longer than they are broad. They emphazise three-dimensional fullness and thereby attain a vitality, and inner force, that does not come from the model. All this, however, is in harmony with the material used for these sculptures, which is wood.

When we read Moore's later statements, Roger Fry's words spring to mind. They unquestionably served as a signpost showing him where to search for knowledge and in what direction to develop his own powers. Everyone finds what he needs; if this concept of sculpture had not already lain dormant in him, Fry's words would have fallen on stony ground.

In the first place, he was impressed by the principle of truth to material. From childhood on he had been interested in material, above all in stone, stone as such and the working of stone. In a speech at a congress organized by UNESCO (Venice 1952) Moore said: "Some become sculptors because they like using their hands, or because they love particular materials, wood or stone, clay or metal, and like working in these materials — that is, they like the craft of sculpture — I do." Then he spoke of the other preconditions for the creation of sculpture. But as a world-famous sculptor of fifty-four he did not hesitate to refer to the emotion that seized him when, as a beginner, he came face to face with the naked materials of his craft ('The Artist in Contemporary Society', UNESCO, 1954).

Moore found himself fully in 1922, when he won a competition and was able to exchange Leeds for London, the Leeds School of Art for the Royal College of Art. There he had good teachers — he remembers Leon Underwood with gratitude — and entered a circle of people who encouraged him. During his first year in London he began to work independently; the sculpture 'Mother and Child' of 1922 is a closed and shut-in composition that extricates itself laboriously from the block of stone. In 1923 he already produced introverted half-length figures and heads in wood and terracotta, in 1924 another 'Mother and Child' and a conventional 'Torso' in plaster for bronze which he later destroyed. Then came a pause. In 1925 Moore was appointed lecturer in sculpture at the Royal College; in 1926 he went on a travelling scholarship to Paris, Rome, Florence, Venice and Ravenna; it was his first major trip abroad and it enabled him to check and supplement on the spot impressions he had received on his visits to the London museums, particularly the British Museum with its abundant collections of ancient oriental, Greek, and pre-Columbian sculpture.

Though Moore did not keep a diary, from which we should learn more about the decisive impressions he received in London, various facts emerge from his later essays. But even if we did not have these documents we could, up to a point, deduce his "teachers" from his works. The 20th-century artist acquires fundamental concepts outside the Academies; the latter can teach him his craft, but not that which lies byond it. It is certain that from the very beginning the classical and the Graeco-Roman did not exist for Moore, and Paul Gauguin's lapidary dictum also seems to apply to him: "Bear the Persians in mind, the people of Cambodia and a little the Egyptians. The great error is Greek art, beautiful though it is. We must go far back, much farther than the Parthenon — as far as the 'dada' of our childhood, the good old wooden hobby-horse." It is noteworthy that Maillol, who appears to us the embodiment of the Mediterranean, wrote as though continuing this dictum: "Negro art contains more ideas than Greek art. We are no longer able to take those liberties so successfully taken by the Negroes. We are too subservient to the past." And he calls Praxiteles the Bouguereau of sculpture and the first hack.

We are too subservient to the past, a particular past, Moore would have added, which through the idea of humanism has become a façade. All the same, no artist can do without a past; the question is, which past he attaches himself to. He does not have a free choice, if he is a true artist and not an eclectic. An "inner necessity" directed and guided Moore, on his visits to the British Museum, to the ancient and mythological. The culminating points of the high civilisations did not interest him, neither biblical Babylon, nor the Amarna period of Egypt, nor the masterpieces of Phidias; he was drawn to the essential vitality of beginnings, to the dream, not to harmony, to vigour, not to beauty. It was almost thirty years before, confronted by the Parthenon on his trip to Greece in 1951, he grasped the meaning of classicism, which still contains the germ of its origins. A moment of historical importance for the world, but only a moment. The Elgin Marbles in the British Museum had failed to reveal the meaning of Greek sculpture; torn from their context and shown in the light of the banks of the Thames, they had remained alien to him.

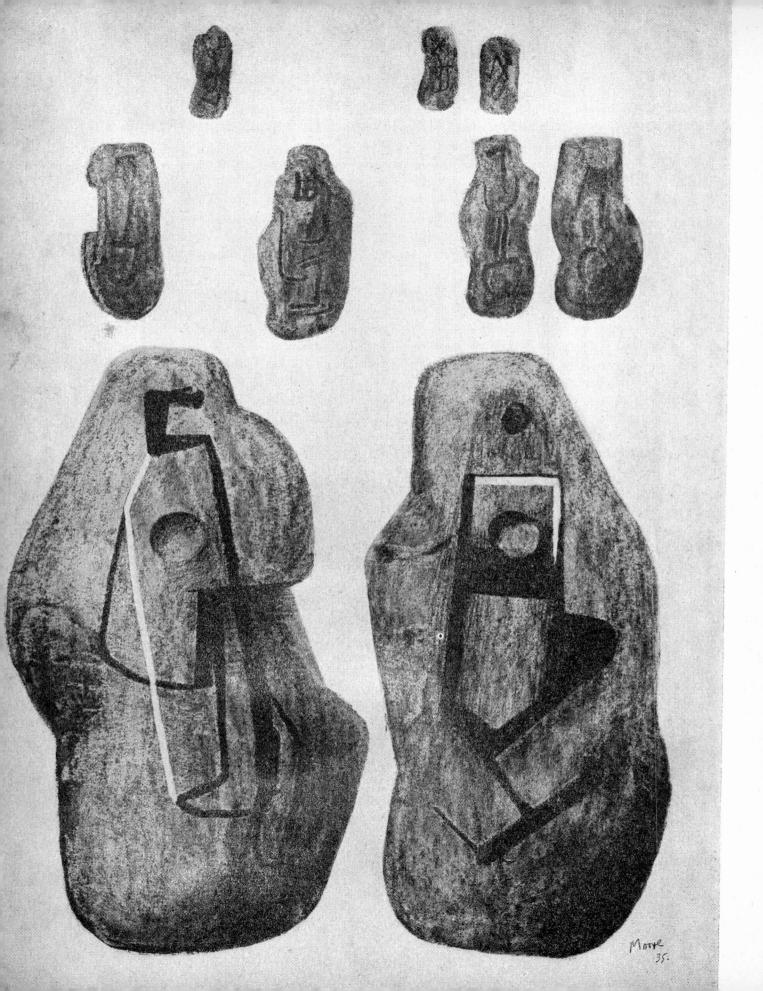

In an essay on 'Primitive Art' (1941) Moore takes us on a "memory-journey" through the British Museum. "At first my visits were mainly and naturally to the Egyptian galleries, for the monumental impressiveness of Egyptian sculpture was nearest to the familiar Greek and Renaissance ideals one had been born to." In the later dynasties, however, Moore finds that this monumental quality wanes, the works lose their appeal and those of later periods seem to him "too stylized and hieratic, with a tendency to academic obviousness". Then he saw the Assyrian reliefs: "— journalistic commentaries and records of royal lion hunts and battles, but beyond was the Archaic Greek room with its lifesize female figures, seated in an easy, still naturalness, grand and full like Handel's music"; the Sumerian sculptures: "Some with a contained bull-like grandeur and held-in energy"; the Old Stone Age: "A lovely tender carving of a girls head, no bigger than one's thumbnail, and beside it female figures of a very human but not copyist realism"; Negro art: "Truth to material... This completer realization of the component parts of the figure gives to Negro carving a more three-dimensional quality than many primitive periods where stone is the main material used. For the Negro, as for other primitive peoples, sex and religion were the two interacting springs of life"; Mexico: "Mexican sculpture, as soon as I found it, seemed to me true and right, perhaps because I at once hit on similarities in it with some 11th-century carvings I had seen as a boy on Yorkshire churches. Its 'stoniness', by which I mean its truth to material, its tremendous power without loss of sensitiveness, its astonishing variety and fertility of form-invention and its approach to a full three-dimensional conception of form, make it unsurpassed in my opinion by any other period of stone sculpture." Mexico, then, made a deep impression on him, and the first 'Reclining Figure' of 1929 is a homage to the 'Rain God', of which, however, he cannot have seen the original, since it stands in Mexico City. Then there were "the New Guinea carvings, the solid stone figures of the Marquesas Islands, the emasculated ribbed figures of Easter Island, the carvings of New Ireland, which have, besides their vicious kind of vitality, a unique spatial sense, a bird-in-a-cage form." Of this multiplicity of manifestations Moore writes: "But underlying these individual characteristics, these featural peculiarities in the primitive schools, a common world-language of form is apparent in them all ... the same shapes and form relationships are used to express similar ideas at widely different places and periods in history ... And on further familiarity with the British Museum's whole collection it eventually becomes clear to me that the realistic ideal of physical beauty in art ... was only a digression from the main world tradition

19

of sculpture, whilst, for instance, our own equally European Romanesque and Early Gothic are in the main line."

This is almost a programme. Moore is unlikely to have seen things quite so clearly at the time as he did in retrospect; in looking back, he undoubtedly apportions relative significance more accurately than he can have done while still a beginner. The choice of essentials from the overwhelming wealth of objects in the British Museum is expert in the extreme, while the reasons for the choice are dictated by the conception of sculpture revealed in his works of 1922.

The logic and consistency of Moore's development will become more evident if we briefly sketch the main ideas advanced in his earliest writings. We can do so all the more readily because Moore is no theorist and writes nothing that he has not experienced in his work and checked hundreds of times. He writes only of his own aims and avoids discussing the ideas and productions of his contemporaries. He is also shy in this respect and when asked to whom he feels close as a sculptor, hesitates to mention a name. Constructional sculpture in steel, iron and other metals is somewhat alien to him, even that by those younger British sculptors who have worked as assistants in his studio. As a member of the working committee (though not of the jury) of the international competition for a Monument to the Unknown Political Prisoner (1953), he was very restrained. He always stands up for his own ideas, but would never make a yardstick of himself.

In his writings on art, he stresses, to begin with, his primary concern with the material (see his statement in the 'Architects' Association Journal', 1930, and in 'Unit One', 1934. In Moore's view, a stone carving must frankly look like stone; to make it look like a being of flesh and blood is mere sleight of hand. The sculptor must work directly in the material for only then can it play its part in moulding his ideas. Contrary to his later utterances, Moore here draws a distinction between carving and modelling, like Adrian Stokes in 'The Stones of Rimini' (London 1934). Stokes writes: "A figure carved in stone is fine carving when one feels that not the figure, but the stone through the medium of the figure has come to life. Plastic conception on the other hand is uppermost when the material with which, or from which, a figure has been made, appears no more than as so much suitable stuff for this creation" (quoted by J. J. Sweeney, 'Henry Moore', New York 1946).

This distinction is justified and clarifies many misunderstandings, but even for Moore it soon became too restrictive. For he, too, came in the course of time to modelling for bronze and cement casts and to making terracottas. As his compositions increased in variety, the indirect method forced itself upon him, the result alone can decide in each case whether the means have been correct.

20

As Moore knows, it is not enough to be true to the material; the work must also be three-dimensional, if it is to be a genuine sculpture. It must be fully rounded; that is to say, all the various members of the form must be fully realized and operate as opposed masses: they must stretch, expand and thrust, only then will they awaken the block to the complete formal existence of a composition, a totality enveloped by air. Sculpture fully in the round has no two views alike. "The desire for form completely realized is connected with asymmetry... Asymmetry is connected also with the desire for the organic (which I have) rather than the geometric. Organic forms, though they may be symmetrical in their main disposition, in their reaction to environment, growth and gravity, lose their perfect symmetry."

What Moore seeks to realize could also be accomplished within the realm of the abstract, for organic and abstract are related at their roots. Moore keeps to the organic, because he does not wish to renounce the vital force that is at work in nature as in the artist.

Moore thereby moves beyond the elemental and reaches out from the domain of material and special problems to that of spiritual and absolute values. What is it that he wishes to realize and how? He certainly does not wish to depict nature, but, equally certainly to him "the observation of nature is part of an artist's life", it enriches the artists's knowledge of form and preserves him from 'working only by formula'. Although it is the human figure which interests him most deeply, he discovers "principles of form and rhythm from the study of natural objects such as pebbles, rocks, bones, trees, plants etc". Pebbles show nature's way of working stone, rocks have restless, massive rhythm, bones wonderful structural power and hard formal tension, trees illustrate the fundamental laws of growth, shells the hollow shape of nature. Moore finds the same laws that have developed out of the germ cell in all the realms of nature; inspiration itself comes in the first place from nature; nature teaches fundamental principles like balance, rhythm, organic growth, attraction and repulsion, harmony and contrast. Moore knows therefore that appearance is only a part of the whole and that the invisible is more important than the accident of that which can be perceived by the eye.

But the most important thing is still missing, the inner vision and the power of expression. Character and psychological elements are reflected in the elemental principles, form comes from within and from a considerable depth, is no more arbitrary than it is imitative, "presents the human psychological content", and above and beyond this comes to terms with something that is more than individual. Moore calls it the initial idea; perhaps it is the "ideal form" in Plato's sense, perhaps merely that which lies beyond perception (Kant) and he wishes to combine the abstract principles of sculpture as intensely as possible with the realisation of this idea. "All art is an

abstraction to some degree... Abstract qualities of design are essential to the value of a work, but to me of equal importance is the psychological, human element. If both abstract and human elements are welded together in a work, it must have fuller, deeper meaning."

The artist is often a philosopher, and Moore philosophizes from the viewpoint of his craft; he thinks of the combination of plastic form with a particular view of the world, which in him is something like life itself. He speaks again and again of the work's fullness of life, of its restrained energy, of the powerful vitality it may have, independently of the object. "When a work has this powerful vitality, we do not connect the word Beauty with it. Beauty, in the later Greek or Renaissance sense, is not the aim in my sculpture." Even if the work be far removed from nature, it can be more real than nature, thrust deeper into nature and contain the essential meaning of life. Somewhat later, in 1937, Moore speaks of the "associational psychological factors" in sculpture. "Round forms convey an idea of fruitfulness, maturity, probably because the earth, women's breasts and most fruits are rounded, and these shapes are important because they have this background in our habits of perception." And he begins, at first rather hesitantly, to think about space. The spectator should comprehend form in its full spatial existence. The sculptor must strive continually to think of, and use, form in its full spatial completeness; he realizes its volume as the space that the shape displaces in the air. He knows while he looks at one side what the other side is like. These thoughts touch upon the most acute problems with which Henry Moore had to grapple during the early years of his work.

A sculptor who brings nothing with him but his talent and the wish to make something of it, but has little opportunity of widening his field of vision, can succeed only if he has a strong will and also some luck. That Moore found Roger Fry's book in Leeds was luck, though it may also have been instinct; that he came to London and the Royal College was already the reward of his intense efforts. He must have attracted attention, for what he produced at the age of twenty-three was a great deal more than a student's work. At this turning point, he burnt all his bridges behind him and embarked on his true career.

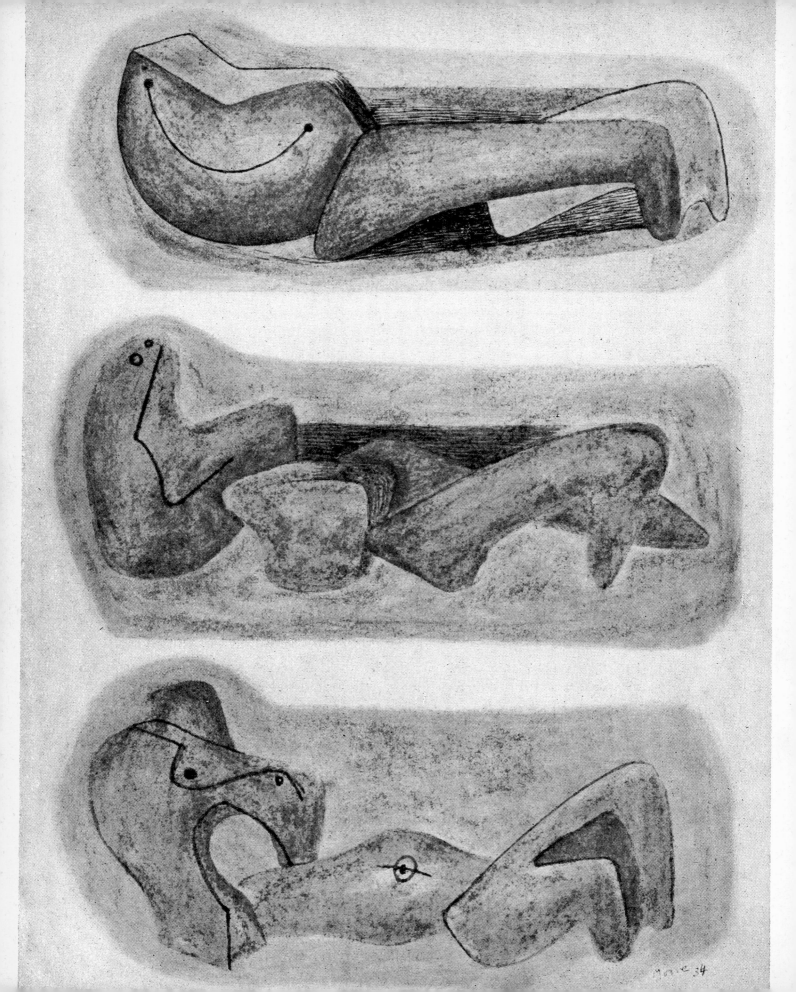

## THE FIRST TEN YEARS (1922—1932)

The 'Mother and Child' (1922, stone, Plate 3) is paradigmatic in its massiveness and weightiness. The closed-in nature of the stone is over-emphasized, the limbs are un-articulated, of the child only the head and hands are visible in high relief, so that any breaking-up of the solid block is avoided. This is the unacademic work of a beginner. It is hard to say how much of it is influenced by the primitives in the British Museum and how much it expresses Moore's own ideas. Moore was slightly behind the times as the painters of German "Brücke" group and the "Fauves" (Matisse, Derain) had already produced comparable sculptures ten to fifteen years ahead of him. But the younger man was to catch up with giant strides. The second version of 'Mother and Child' (1924, stone, Plate 4) is already more articulated and more closely related to the theme of mother, child, fertility. The heavy masses of the body, unlike the work of 1922, are rounded off on all sides and overlap one another in a concentric arrangement. The powerful right arm rises like a protecting wall in front of the mother's face. The child is enthroned on her shoulders and bends heavily forward over her forehead, with cubic forms that contrast with the round organic shapes of the woman. There is a wealth of flat and twisted planes, determined more by the original block of stone than by the artist's will. He may have seen crowned construc-tions among Mexican works ('Maize Goddess'), similar except that their burden is displaced even more definitely upwards. Most Mexican of all are the two masks (1929, cement, and 1929, stone, Plates 1 and 15). The first is built up, according to the rules of Cubism (here, too, he had to make up for lost time) of sharply carved planes and organized into a general oval shape; the second is moonlike, curved, more human in expression. The astonishing thing is the monumental effect of these early works in relation to their real size, a characteristic that continues in Moore's later works. Anyone who knows them only from photographs will usually imagine them far larger than they are. Another point of interest, present at this period and even more marked later, is the great variety within one work so that it is often diffi-cult to tell whether photographs taken from several angles are really of one and the same sculpture.

The commonest theme during the early years was the 'Mother and Child'; for Moore this is primarily an allegory of the primordial, the womb, fertility, not of tender motherliness. Not until 1929 do warmer emotional elements find their way into the plastic composition. In that year Moore married, and it is reasonable to attribute the psychological transformation of the theme to the change in his way of life, just as a new note appears in his 'Family Groups' after the birth of his daughter in 1946. Not that there is ever anything personal or private in Henry Moore's work but the life of the forms becomes less hard and sharp. In 1928 and 1929 the theme is still an exercise. Moore is experimenting: he plunges the child in the hollow of the breast (the connecting link between inside and outside) or forms a sheltering hollow of the arms or cuts the composition off at the hips, so that the whole construction is removed from the realm of the humanly natural. On one occasion he places the child against the breast; another time he puts it at a distance, or he fuses the limbs of the two beings into a rhythmically harmonious cradle shape; he may seat the child on its mother's hand or stand it on her lap, so that their heads are on the same level. In one of his compositions of 1928 the mother is seated on some steps, a theme to which he was to return much later. All these compositions are not mere variations, but each is a new task Moore sets himself. He is preoccupied by the problem of the movement of the arms on their own and in embracing the child, for the function of movement and the way in which the posture of the arms causes the whole composition to vibrate, without disturbing its static balance, are important considerations. The three-quarter-length figure of 1931 (stone, Plate 7) places the child, which is encircled by the over-long arms of the mother, spatially at the level of the breasts; the neck is a column like the lower part of the body, the head a slightly indented sphere, but the twist of the arms imparts movement to the squarely frontal pose.

Moore does not allow himself to become enslaved by his guiding principles; while he is creating sculptures that are true to material and three-dimensional and expanding his knowledge of formal plastic factors, he also studies nature, occasionally through the medium of clay models which he afterwards destroyed but more often by means of numerous drawings. At one time he used to draw and carve contemporaneously; later he gave this up, because he found that the one hindered the other. If the drawing was too complete a representation of the sculpture to be, it weakened his desire to do the sculpture or tended to make the sculpture only a "dead representation of the drawing". In later years he left a wider latitude to the drawings, often drawing in line and flat tone without the illusion of three dimensions; to begin with, however, he found drawing "a useful outlet for ideas which there is not time enough to realize as a sculpture". He also uses drawings as a method of study and observation of natural forms (drawings from life, drawings of bones, shells, etc.). Moore, who cannot dispense with the organic and morphological, studies nature and enriches his canon of forms, without losing sight of the original impulses, material and three-dimensionality. Just as he exercises his powers of observation by drawing, so he develops his judgment by reading. Particularly after his visit to Italy in 1925 he became responsive to art books, with whose help he recalled what he had seen. The weightiness of the 'Mother and Child' of 1932 (stone, Sainsbury Collection) is almost unthinkable without deep penetration into the spirit of Michelangelo.

We can see best how his observations benefited his work in the standing figures; in the 'Young Girl' (1931, stone, Plate 8) — one of the many standing figures in three-quarter view — it appears in the position of the hands, the expression of the eyes. There is great sensibility of expression in the way the arms gently touch one another and the right hand the breast in the almost classical figure in Armenian marble (1932, Plate 12). There are also similar figures in wood which are more elongated, taller, smoother because of the material. The little alabaster figure of 1931 (Plate 10) is by comparison hard and chunky. Moore here switches over to a more shut-in emotional scale, a process that is nothing unusual with him. He likes the polarity of cold and warm, closed and open, complicated and simple; life is both and so is art. Two concentric circles on the head indicate eyes, a face. Moore is opposed to graphic aids, but not to the introduction of indications that more clearly approach the plane of absolutes like mass, rhythm and weight than explanatory appendages. It is worth noting how Moore avoids symmetry; the left arm displaces the axis, the little buttonlike head, the alteration of the scale of the limbs, "fools" our idea of proportion.

A stronger tendency to asymmetry marks the 'Head and Shoulders' (1927, marble, Plate 5), a face divided in two with contrasting eyes and flattened forehead, the left shoulder drawn up and massive, as though in defence, the other sloping away and disappearing into the right breast. The energy thrusting out from within threatens to burst the shell.

By 1929 Moore had become conscious of the need to combine the inner and outer elements in construction and expression. In the 'Figure in Cement' (1929, Plate 6) he tears open the breast, which rests like a shrine in the enclosure of the body in an attempt to break open the shell, to force space into the representation and make it take an active part in fashioning it. The problem is difficult, and Moore did not entirely succeed in breaking through from one side to the other until later, in the alabaster carving of 1935 (Plate 11). This abstract formation, behind which a half-length figure is probably concealed, stands before us like a stone washed out by the sea. Moore causes the mass not merely to displace space, but to draw space, hollow space, into the sculptural composition as an active element. Form is here conceived "in its full spatial completeness", as "forms in space", as an identity between space and form, with the limitation that space cannot take the place of form, for "form is heavy". This figure brings sculpture close to Peruvian jugs or Bronze Age domestic urns, as though volume around the hollow space was now also a receptacle. That the hollowness therefore has the effect of fullness is an inexplicable dialectic, but with Moore it remains within the framework of the organic and the humanly meaningful. He was to revert to this problem again later.

Moore's activities during the first ten years spread out in all directions; he was over-flowing with sculptural ideas and struggling to realize them. Not every attempt was successful and he destroyed a good deal of his work, but most of it served as a first step towards more mature solutions. In 1928 he received his first commission, a relief for the headquarters of the London Underground Railway, a horizontal flying female figure, 'North Wind', the legs of which are so thickened that they look like heavy clouds. The same year he held his first one-man exhibition, at the Warren Gallery, London, encouraged by the sculptor Jacob Epstein, then an important figure in the artistic life of London. Moore became known to a small circle of art lovers. He was also still active as a teacher at the Royal College of Art, where he had been a student and where he taught until 1932. From 1932 to 1939 he was on the staff of the Chelsea School of Art. Teaching is not a waste of time for him; like all good teachers he learns from his pupils and especially from the necessity of formulating clearly much that he had known only intuitively.

The problem of the 'Seated Figure' emerged in 1929; so did that of the 'Head' seen not as a portrait, but as a theme. Only in one alabaster head from 1929 does the spectator think of a portrait. There are also a few animal sculptures from this period that suggest Chinese art, the 'Snake' for example, and also a few works that are moving in the direction of abstraction, such as the composition in walnut of 1932. Moore's achievement during the first decade is all the more considerable when we bear in mind that he was working in a comparatively sterile artistic climate which was not in the least encouraging. He entered the briefer second phase, which was cut short by the outbreak of the Second World War, with a feeling that he could continue to build upon what he had acquired; he now knew his materials — stone of varying degrees of hardness, wood, cement, terracotta, clay; he had become clear in his own mind about the basic elements of his craft, about mass, volume, dimension and space and also about the range of his predetermined themes, among them the 'Mother and Child', which occupies first place, and next to this the woman, standing and sitting, as a bust and as a half- or three-quarter-length figure. Only the repre-sentation of "man" is entirely absent: the structure and mind of man, the being detached from nature, is so foreign to him that representing him can hardly have entered Moore's consciousness. One theme however, has been omitted from this list, the theme that had already begun to preoccupy him during this decade and still absorbs him today: that is the 'Reclining Figure', the woman lying back on her elbows. It touches the deepest chords of his being and leads him as a sculptor from task to task, from solution to solution. For this reason we shall deal with it on its own, independently of the various phases in his creative evolution.

Moore/37.

2

3

4

5

7

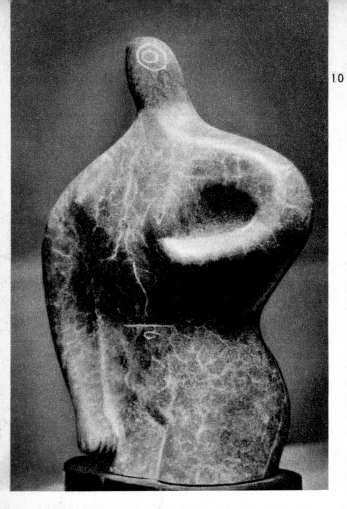

10

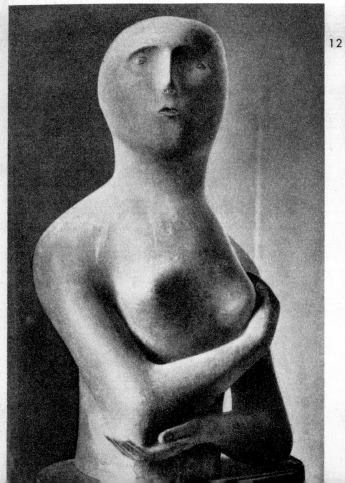

12

## THE RECLINING FIGURE (1929—1958)

There must be reasons why the theme of the 'Reclining Figure' has preoccupied Moore throughout his life; the first two date from 1929, the latest was installed in front of the UNESCO building in 1958. There are two earlier 'Reclining Figures', one in plaster for bronze from 1926 and one in cement from 1927, both initially modelled in clay and naturalistic in style, but these have nothing to do with the theme as Moore developed it later. This begins in 1929 with the 'Reclining Figure' in albaster (Plate 19) and the 'Reclining Figure' in brown Hornton stone (Plate 17).

Looking at these sculptures, we sense Moore's love of nature, the "concrétion humaine" and at the same time his awareness of his own capacities and insights: material, complete three-dimensionality, idea, vitality, the associational psychological factors. "Rounded forms convey an idea of fruitfulness," he writes. He has penetrated deep into the concrete expression of reality, into its organic whole, and equally deeply into the basic elements of sculpture; he has a feeling for the interplay of formal energies. But to explain the powerful effect his sculpture has on us, we have to seek another element: something impersonal, something that goes beyond the temporary instant and also exceeds the boundaries of our age. Access to the 'Reclining Figures' is not blocked, but nor is it open unless we grasp the fact that the artist is in unconscious contact with deeper levels of the human spirit, levels that extend beyond the times we live in and are linked with our beginnings and their symbolic mode of expression. These 'Reclining Figures' are not the reclining women of a Maillol or a Matisse: they are women in repose but also something more profound. We recall Goethe's description of the symbol, which is the thing, without being the thing: "an image concentrated in a mirror and yet identical with the object."

Symbol of what? Of the woman as the concept of fruitfulness, the Mother Earth. Moore, who once pointed to the maternal element in the 'Reclining Figures', may well see in them an element of eternity, the "Great Female", who is both birth-giving nature and the wellspring of the unconscious. In the artist the unconscious is more highly developed than in others; he is dependent upon his ability to receive inspiration from the creative unconscious and is inclined to identify himself with the latter and through it with the maternal as such. To Henry Moore, the 'Reclining Figures' are no mere external objects, he identifies himself with them, as well as the earth and the whole realm of motherhood.

The 'Reclining Figure', then, ceases to be merely one theme among many and becomes a central problem in Moore's creative activity. As part of the basic theme of womanhood that he deals with again and again always differently, the series of 'Reclining Figures' continues uninterrupted throughout all Moore's development as a sculptor, almost like a mirror image. The composition grows increasingly mature and in recent years achieves a transcendent quality, has entered the realm of the numinous. Neither pagan nor Christian, these figures are neutral forms in which nature and spirit meet in accordance with their own laws. The pendulum swings now in one direction, now in the other, pointing at one moment towards the physical, the fruitful, the earthy and at another to the awakening of the unconscious, to spirit, to inner law. The forms are therefore rooted not exclusively in individual creation but at the same time in something superior and collective. The outward shape may equally well be abstract or naturalistic, depending on the extent to which the artist wishes to communicate directly or along the roundabout route of interpretation.

The alabaster figures of 1929 (Plate 19) looks like a relief, in spite of the pronounced indentations between the arms and the marked emphasis of the limbs, because of the projections and the forward twist of the planes. The other 'Reclining Figure' of that year (Plate 17), which is unquestionably connected with the Maya sculpture of Chac-Mool from Chichén-Itzá (Yukatan), is more consciously frontal in pose, but designed to bring the opposed masses more clearly into movement. The Chac-Mool, incidentally, has become a goddess, and one with superhuman features. The head resembles Mexican masks that have this same quality. The way the upper part of the body forms a rectangle by means of the arms contrasts sharply with the slant of the large left thigh. The breasts are strikingly small in relation to the heavy masses of the limbs rising and falling like a mountain range and diverting attention from the figure's essential femaleness. The carving is remarkably static and is, as Moore demands in his statement of 1930, "strong and vital, giving out something of the energy and power of great mountains". This is the maternal seen as Mother Earth, the personal as an anonymous occurrence, the ideal as the divine.

From 1930 on, Moore alternated between naturalistic, earthy versions of the 'Reclining Figures', and abstract, symbolic ones. This was no vacillation, but a constant shifting of creative emphasis between the organic in its widest sense, and the laws at work within nature. Organic life and the laws behind life constitute the two chief components in every work of art. In one case the world is a meaningful whole permeated by a formative force. In the other, there is at work in the artist an all-embracing concept of form through which all his works are related to a single whole. Moore's figures, whether representational or abstract, are all rooted in the same basic pattern, in a force that pervades the whole work. "The loftiest works of art are at the same time the loftiest works of nature," says Goethe, whose theory of form is still valid today and has found an echo among 20th-century painters.

Moore is as mobile as nature and with rare talent combines inner necessity and creative mobility; the same spirit reigns in even the greatest antitheses. Through this spirit he is linked with both the past and future ages, so that the spectator is inclined to speak in the one case of technology, in the other of archaicisms and regressions. Where particular archaic tendencies become perceptible, they easily can be identified as for example, Sumerian art, or, in Picasso's work as the art of the Cyclades. This does not, however, mean that Moore has borrowed from such sources, but that his subconscious reaches into the furthest regions of time and space.

The contrasts in the 'Reclining Figures' Henry Moore made between 1930 and 1933 are particularly marked. In 1930 the naturalistic carving in Hornton stone (formerly Peter Watson Collection) is a humanization of the "Mexican" tendencies in the sculpture of 1929; the next year contrasting elements appear in the 'Reclining Figure' cast in lead (in the Frederick Zimmerman Collection, New York, Plate 20). Constructivistically invented parts, introduced for the first time, are combined with a deformed organic shape. In 1932 Moore produced an almost baroque 'Reclining Figure', carved in concrete (Plate 18, City Art Museum, St Louis). It is followed, in 1933, by a figure leaning back (concrete, Washington University, St Louis), that looks like a draped scaffold, with rods as spatial constructions. Where the treatment is abstract, that which lies within the scope of association—hints of head, arms, body—is not intended to reproduce nature, but to signal it. Yet life is never lacking. To speak of distortion is not quite correct; it would be more appropriate in more realistic works, where a natural element is exaggerated. Here we have self-assertion on the part of the artist, who, as the work proceeds, has to take into account what has gone before and what is to come, if he wishes to capture the whole truth.

From 1933 to 1937 Moore stresses abstraction. It is a different kind of abstraction from that of the mature Kandinsky, more like that of the "Blaue Reiter" group, where the mountains and tree trunks, the rainbows and riders could be felt behind the abstractions. The forms are too autonomous and too filled with their own life to be mere distortions or simplifications. They are not artificial constructions, but fundamental shapes, such as nature itself fashions and which come to life within the sculptor, much as they do in nature through its creative potentials. These forms have many meanings, many things can be read into them, because they are, so to speak, still in the process of becoming. With sculptors like Pevsner or Max Bill we should look for laws whose ultimate expression is numerical as the sources of form, with Moore we seek the primal cause that has interested him from the beginning. In his eyes, stones and shells are also living organisms, in which nature reveals itself, but the human form occupies such a central position that it finds an echo in even the most abstract works.

In the 'Composition in Four Parts' (alabaster, 1934, Plate 22) one may see at first only disjointed pieces without connection, but then one becomes aware of a structure composed of interrelated forms, and only at the very end does one grasp the fact that this work, too, is a reclining figure. Moore expressly states this in its sub-title, which arouses the association of a torso and a head (the spheres), while the bridge-like pieces appear as limbs. It is not wilful destructiveness or distortion or abstraction that breaks the figure into pieces. Moore liberates pure basic shapes and combines them. What interests him is not whether they represent an object, but how they function. There are also lines inscribed on the torso, which may be read as indications of breasts, so that here again we are reminded of the female body. The 'Composition' in concrete, made the same year (Plate 21), is rather more complex. The pierced thorax is more closely connected with the limbs—the arms and legs are not detached. In these works Henry Moore experiments with the process through which volume becomes form and pursues it to its very origins. From them, through the accidental present appearance, he proceeds to the invention of shapes that are living beings and living beings that are within the realm of possibility.

In contrast, the archaic 'Reclining Figure' of 1935 (Plate 23) is reminiscent of Bronze Age domestic urns or better, perhaps, of a coffin, like that of the 17th-dynasty Egyptian king Atnef in the British Museum. The face is a hollow sunk into the head, the ridge of the longitudinal axis is asymmetrically displaced, the hump at the lower end represents the feet. Man and coffin, life and death become one; the beginning and end meet. "I can live just as well among the dead as among the living, rather closer to the heart of creation," Klee once said, that is, to the source, from which all forms and all metamorphoses come.

Then, in 1936, began the series which was to continue uninterrupted until 1939. To it belong some of his most powerful and significant reclining figures. The small figure in the Onslow-Ford Collection (1938, bronze, Plate 25), the model for the large wood carving of 1939 in the same collection, is typical of all the works in bronze or lead of this period (Plates 26, 31—34). None of them is much more than a foot long. Moore also worked in clay, which permits his imagination greater play. As in drawing, he is freer in clay than when he is working directly in the material. As he works the sculptor "gets the solid shape, as it were, inside his head—he thinks of it as if he were holding it completely enclosed in the hollow of his hand. He mentally visualizes a complex form from all round itself ... He identifies himself with its centre of gravity." In the last analysis, Moore does this all the time, but he does so most intensely when he is working in wood and stone. Clay instead gives him greater opportunity for experiment since he is less committed to what he has done and can destroy the model and start again, or change it, if he is not satisfied. Small pieces are not necessarily less important or less effective; "a small carving only a few inches in height can give the feeling of huge size and monumental grandeur, because the vision behind it is big ... The average in-between size does not disconnect an idea enough from prosaic everyday life. The very small or the very big take on an added size emotion." This is an accurate observation which explains why so many lifesize sculptures, particularly in open-air exhibitions, look small and petty, and Moore always thinks of his works as being exhibited out of doors, not in a museum or a private house. He wishes to see them as part of the landscape and remarks that "if practical considerations allowed me, ... I should like to work on large carvings more often than I do."

The small bronzes are the product of his experiences in the more abstract domain; they have greater freedom of invention and are more completely worked out than the large versions in the Tate Gallery and the Onslow-Ford collection. The bronzes have not the bulk of Moore's stone carvings, but they have the same vitality; only in them this vitality is split up so that it does not gravitate towards a centre, but radiates outwards into the bonelike structure and into space (see colour plate page 57). The problem of space had long interested Moore, but previously he had dealt more or less fully with it by means of volumes. Now he opens up the forms, bores holes in the material, removes whole sections of organic life in order to intensify the organic representation. "A piece of stone can have a hole through it and not be weakened—if the hole is of a studied size, shape and direction. On the principle of the arch, it can remain just as strong. The first hole made through a piece of stone is a revelation. The hole connects one side to the other, making it immediately more three-dimensional. A hole can itself have as much shape-meaning as a solid mass. Sculpture in air is possible, where the stone contains only the hole, which is the intended and considered form. The mystery of the hole—the mysterious fascination of caves in hillsides and cliffs" (1937). Although this is said with stone in mind, its analysis of space applies equally to clay and bronze. The hole is the intended form and the stone contains it.

In the execution, the bronzes vary greatly. Some have perforated heads, others cloven heads or heads like saddles; the breasts show positive and negative shapes; the torso is in one case reduced to two linked flat discs, in another to two clasps whose knots suggest breasts; in the lead figure in the Museum of Modern Art, New York, only the spine is left of the torso. A drawing of 1938 (Plate 28) introduces fresh variations on this theme, and in the background four wall drawings that mysteriously prefigure the 'Time and Life' sculptures of 1951; the arms are in some cases like the handles of jugs, in others connective lineations (that, too, are within the realm of possibility); the arms may remain enclosed by the total form or rest like the uprights of scaffolding upon the ground. In the bronzes, light constitutes an active though not as dominant an element as in Brancusi's sculpture, where it is included in the formal plan from the outset and is intensified through a special method of polishing.

Some of the drawings from these years go beyond the sculptural works. In them the 'Reclining Figures' may even look like locusts or other insects but they always suggest something natural, never anything mechanical. Hints of interior or exterior walls already appear in some drawings of 1938 although Moore did not incorporate them in his sculptural work until 1956. The watercolour drawing of 1942 (colour plate page 149) is an echo of these earlier drawings.

The comparatively larger 'Reclining Figure' of Hopton Wood stone at Domfret, Connecticut (1937, Plate 27), is unique in that it successfully and impressively translates all the imaginative plastic ideas of the bronzes into stone. The whole looks something like a large shoe, with a cap in the front, like the hump in the sarcophagus-shaped 'Reclining Figure' of 1935, an upward-looking, moonlike face and a suggestion of breasts and pelvis, but limbless.

The large carvings of this period are relatively naturalistic: one in Buffalo (elm wood, 1936, Albright Art Gallery), one in Wakefield (elm wood, 1936, City Art Gallery), and the one illustrated here which is in the Tate Gallery, London (green Hornton stone, 1938, Plate 30). The 'Recumbent Figure' in the Tate Gallery is a huge modelled sphere; the arms and legs, which pass imperceptibly one into the other, breast and arms so natural one hardly notices the opening; the head is a barely modelled sphere; the arms and legs, which pass imperceptibly one into the other, make up the overall undulating shape.

The wood carving in the Onslow-Ford Collection (1939, Plate 29) is the most evolved and exciting of them all. If we look at it with the head foremost, we are drawn almost forcibly into the vast cavern of the torso. The hollow is the form, framed by the limbs, which, however, are so open that looked at lengthways the sculpture appears as a grid of thick swellings. At all points it leads from within outwards into space. It does not look the same from any two viewpoints and in Protean fashion, changes as we look at it, as though it were "a figure in progress"; this is all the more astonishing because, as a physical phenomenon, the hollow ought to impose stability and rest. It draws the spectator into its darkness, into its womb, but the interior is also an opening that leads back into the light. Along the surface of the wood, a surface marked by growth and life, the eye moves, from front to back as though through a labyrinth. Before the onlooker can apprehend its parts, he must discover that inside and outside are indistinguishable, and that the carving is a single whole.

The material of wood plays a considerable role in this process, for it has a life of its own, at one moment meeting the artist half way, at another thwarting his intentions; here it determines the course taken by the forms, there it interrupts it. The sculptor, however, thinks not only in terms of the material; he must also oppose his will to it and thus decide the course to be taken and the final form achieved. By so doing he sets his activity off from participation in the present.

From 1939 to 1945, the theme of the 'Reclining Figure' sank into the background. Since 1932, Moore had owned, besides his London studio, a small house in Kent, where he could work in the open. After the outbreak of war he moved into the country altogether which was all the more easy for him as he had given up teaching that year. In 1940, however, he returned to London and as Official War Artist was commissioned to draw the people in London's air raid shelters. His studio was partially destroyed, and in 1940 he moved to Much Hadham, where he has lived ever since. In 1941 became a trustee of the Tate Gallery, an appointment that was renewed in 1949 for another seven years. In 1945 he became an honorary doctor of Leeds University. In 1943 he was commissioned to make a 'Virgin and Child' for St Matthew's Church, Northampton, and completed the work in 1944. Even the war years were filled with work; he did not produce much sculpture, but countless drawings and watercolours, the shelter drawings, the drawings of miners in the pits and also preliminary studies for the 'Family Groups' and the 'Helmets'. These were displayed in the big exhibition at the Museum of Modern Art, New York, which took place shortly after the war (1946) and for the opening of which Moore travelled to the United States. In this year his daughter Mary was born. The number of exhibitions increased from year to year, as did the honours, and he became a member or an honorary member of several scientific and artistic institutions—in 1953 an honorary doctor of London University, in 1958 honorary doctor of Harvard University, in 1959 honorary doctor of Cambridge. In 1955 he became a trustee of the National Gallery, London. He won prizes for sculpture at Venice in 1948, São Paulo in 1953, Pittsburgh (Carnegie Institute) in 1958, Tokyo in 1959. In 1957 he was awarded the Stefan Lochner Medal by the city of Cologne.

The war years prevented the execution of so many plans initiated during the 1930s that we do not know what might have merged from these projects if their development had proceeded undisturbed. But the 'Reclining Figure' theme cropped up again almost immediately after the war, continued almost uninterrupted to 1953 and attained its culmination so far in the UNESCO sculpture of 1958. There are larger and smaller versions, once more in many materials, and frequently the smaller ones are preliminary stages of the monumental ones. At the beginning of 1945 he made two clay models for the 'Memorial' at Dartington Hall (in 1946 the monument itself was executed in green Hornton stone), in 1945 three models for the great 'Reclining Figure' that belonged to Curt Valentin, New York, and is now in the Cranbrook Academy of Art, Michigan, in 1946 a terracotta study for the 'Reclining Figure' in stone in the Ingersoll Collection, Philadelphia (executed in 1949), in 1947 the 'Reclining Figure' in the H. R. Hope Collection, Indiana, and in 1950 the huge bronze in the Musée d'Art Moderne, Paris. In 1951 Moore modelled the design for the 'Reclining Figure (Inner and Outer Forms)', which he carried out in 1953 and 1954, and after a few further compositions on a small scale he produced the 'Draped Reclining Figure' for the 'Time and Life' building in London (1952/3). The UNESCO carving did not come into being until five years later. Moore's capacity for work was increasing year by year and alongside the 'Reclining Figures', he produced works on entirely new and different lines.

The Dartington 'Memorial' (Plate 38) has been described as classical and so have the 'Three Standing Figures' for Battersea Park, London. They are unquestionably different in style from the wood carving at Cranbrook. His public often expects the artist to be immediately recognizable and not to disappoint the expectations derived from his previous works. But a memorial may very well spring from quite different levels of experience and plastic vision and the mastery over stone may occasionally lead to constructions that are less earthy, that verge on the classical, and hence approach beauty which Moore does not characterize as "his task". There is not a trace of classicism in this sculpture, however, and its "decorative" quality is, in the French sense, an expression of consummate ability.

'Reclining Figure' in wood (Plates 39, 40), which has been displayed in all Moore's major exhibitions and has attracted much attention, contrasts with the 'Memorial' although made at the same time. As in the wood carving in the Onslow-Ford Collection, Moore is here possessed by an urge to penetrate the block of wood that at the same time bound up with the mental image of the mysterious and unknown world of motherhood. It is more of an exorcism than an idea. A shudder runs through the spectator who wanders into this region "where images of all creatures hover around him", as it says in Part Two of Goethe's 'Faust'. The incisions, the hollows and the perforations in the wood are encroachments upon a life process, that having something dictatorial about them. The sculptor leads, but he is also led; the swelling volumes of the neck and chest, and of the left thigh, are gigantic shapes that lie closer to nature than to consciousness. They are mountains, such as Moore has long seen in his mind's eye, a union of landscape and sculpture.

The 'Reclining Figure' in the Hope Collection (1947, stone, Plates 41, 42) is closer to the Dartington 'Memorial' than to the wood carvings. In the closed body space is created only through the bent limbs. The smooth contours of the softly modelled

volumes flow away and close up again. The creaturely element predominates. In the Ingersoll sculpture (1949, stone, Plate 43), which is so full of movement, the mass of the diagonally constructed body billows out like a sail, and the shallow indentation in the hollow of the breast follows the gesture of the arms; the left thigh stretches across to the abdomen like a bridge and counterbalances the bulky support of the right arm. Here the bronze model (1946) shows how intensely Moore works on his preliminary studies; what in the latter is still naturalistically mobile, and emphasized by linear additions, in the final version becomes a state of powerful repose.

In the terrifying 'Reclining Figure' in the Musée d'Art Moderne, Paris (1951, bronze, Plates 44, 45; preliminary study, bronze 1950), Moore has returned to the abstract compositions of the 1930s (see Plate 26) and the non-figurative works at the end of the war (see Plate 35). It is the culmination of the series of non-naturalistic configurations that represent a symbiosis between nature and ghostly spectres. We think as much of gigantic prehistoric beasts, as of human beings, much as in the bronzes of the 1930s. Whether this 'Reclining Figure' is an incarnation of evil rather than of good, of death rather than of life, is not easy to decide, but despite the hollow structure, it does not belong to the "hollow man" species. Its majesty is unmistakable; it stretches straight up, rests upon the wedge of the arms and thrusts powerfully off with its shin bones; its vitality lies in the immense tension that runs from the base of the feet to the head, whose cleavage indicates conflict, the "age of anxiety". The frightening figure reveals its meaning most clearly when seen from the side and back, for there the hollow shapes form the entrance to a kingdom of the dead.

Of all Moore's work, the smaller bronzes and terracottas produced after the war are among the richest in spiritual and formal problems. Those of 1945 and 1946 (Plates 25—37) continue the "constructive" works of 1938, but they are not merely further variations on them. In one bronze (Plate 35) two themes are interlocked, the lever running out from the right ear to the chest and the configuration of the arms which give this 'Reclining Figure' its non-human look. Rigidly propped up on its brazen arm supports, the 'Reclining Figure' (Plate 37), which has a hint of engineering about it yet not without magic, is a being from another planet. The watercolour and chalk drawings reproduced on page 51 echo these compositions.

Some years later, between 1952 and 1954, Moore made six smaller bronzes that were all more or less in keeping with organic nature. The 'Reclining Figure' (Plate 56) is an anguished creature gazing into the void, the broken axes strictly framed by the vertical of the right arm and the diagonal of the legs. The half erect figure of 1954 (Plate 59) has something of the priestess about it that suggests a guardian of the entrance to a secret place. A surprising innovation appears in the dresses worn by thin reclining figures which are also related to the 'Leaf Figures'. They are overrefined, worldly persons who contradict everything else that Moore has done (1952, bronze, Plate 58). Again and again he approaches from a new angle the problem of sculptural form and expression and creates a new female type. Henry Moore had been occupied with the question of inside and outside as a spatial and psychological problem ever since the 1930s. Then, from 1951 to 1954, he evolved the conception of a reclining figure in which the kernel and the shell were separated, only to reunite them in the end. In 1951 he made a model for bronze (Plate 46) consisting of a hollow 'Reclining Figure' open in many directions, within which he set a closed figure, the head and neck of which project upward through an opening. Pursuing this idea further, he produced a large model of the interior figure in 1953, which, however, he destroyed. In the end he was left with the cloak composition (Plates 47—49). At the same time Moore produced a composition which he called 'Inner and Outer Forms', of which there is a "working model" dating from 1951, a model in plaster for bronze from 1952/3, and a definitive version in elm wood from 1953/4 (Plates 50, 51). Work on the two compositions, the horizontal 'Reclining Figure' and the vertical 'Inner and Outer Forms', therefore proceeded side by side. Moore approached the task from two points of view and not altogether without preparation, for as long ago as 1940 he had made a 'Standing Figure' with a separate figure inside it and in 1950 two more similar compositions (see Plates 91—94 and colour plate page 109). The colour drawing of the 'Two Upright Figures' (1940, colour plate page 41) also belongs in this context.

What these compositions mean is evident from the interpretation of the 'Reclining Figures' as Mother Earth. The hollow shape is in both cases, although barely recognizable as such, the maternal envelope and the interior form the new life, child or soul. In the last analysis the two are not separated; outside and inside, envelope and enveloped, are identical, a unity of earth and man, bearer and born. The envelope alone, in the last version, with its labyrinthine spatial forms, is so impressive because its expression is less direct, and therefore more symbolic: after the expulsion of the interior form, it becomes the grave.

In 1951 Moore went to Greece and saw Athens, Mycenae, Delphi, Olympia and Corinth. On the verge of fifty, he experiences the world whose 'beauty' he had doubted. The archaic had impressed him as a student when he visited the British Museum, but not Pheidias and still less his successors. He was by now too deeply ensconced in his own personal outlook for the new impressions to change it materially, but sufficiently open to feel them in his own way. The 'Reclining Figure' for the 'Time and Life' building in London (1952/3, bronze, Plates 52—54) is the outcome of an inner sympathy that reveals his identity more clearly than many stubbornly individualistic works. He himself calls this 'Reclining Figure' "a more human and realistic work", which would "have a value as a contrast to the architecture of the building" (1954). In this context he refers to what he learnt from his shelter drawings about the formal function of drapery. Folds are capable of bringing out the tensions of the bodily structure, they can be drawn tight as a bandage over the projecting places (breasts, shoulders, etc.) but the contrast with the slackness of the hanging drapery intensifies the force thrusting out from within. Not "decoration", but accentuation is the aim, and one entirely in accord with Henry Moore's earlier ideas and productions. "Force, Power, is made by forms straining or pressing from inside. Knees, elbows, forehead, knuckles, all seek to press outwards. Hardness, projection outwards, gives tension, force, and vitality . . . Space in sculpture should not become such a fetish that the form is weak and impoverished" (1953). The 'Time and Life' sculpture is a 'Reclining Figure' like the rest, but a goddess, a Persephone of the upper world, who embodies spring in the same way at the Aphrodite and her companion on the east pediment of the Parthenon. The body of the statue, scarcely touching the ground and lightly supported on hands and feet, offers the cradle of its torso to the sun; the body seems to be awakening, waking also the expression of the face. The subtle covering of the 'Draped Torso' (1953, bronze, Plate 55) accentuates even more clearly the intentional interplay of contrasts. It is mainly motivated by a delight in the play of folds and in the differentiation of the surface, which is Moore's way of re-interpreting Classical art.

In the 1950s Moore experimented in many directions and produced a number of works which lie outside the general line of his development though not unconnected with it. Among these is the 'Reclining Figure' of 1956 (bronze, Plate 60), which in the course of further work Moore set on end and mounted against a wall (Plate 61). Another bronze, which he produced while working on the UNESCO figure, is filled, in contrast to the latter, with an "extroverted" dramatic quality. In compositions like these Moore throws off the burden of the superhuman concentration demanded by a work like the 'Reclining Figure' for the UNESCO building in Paris (1957/8, Roman travertine, Plates 63—68).

Moore wavered as to the theme to choose for UNESCO. He took the commission as such more seriously than he usually does. On one of the pages of sketches and

notes for this project he wrote: "Theme: the passing on by humanity of the Education, Science = Culture to the succeeding generations, in the hope that the next generations will both enjoy and employ them better." Below this he has noted: "Mother figure bending towards a child figure, two parent and mother figures with child between them etc." He also considers the idea of a woman seated in front of a wall, of a 'Family Group' such as he had evolved since 1943, and of people reading and arguing. There are drawings showing free-standing figures and figures seated on steps and in front of a background; he also though of a more abstract, empty throne, a kind of "hetoimasia", a place of expectation. He chose a 'Reclining Figure'. The bronze model is 8 ft 4 ins long, the final carving 16 ft 6 ins so that it is his largest work. Moore personally selected the block from the quarries near Rome, from which the stone used for the front of the UNESCO building came, and worked it in the marble quarries of Querceta (winter 1957, spring and summer 1958), at the foot of that same mountain where Michelangelo spent two years breaking up and working his blocks. In Paris Moore merely added the final touches and designed the plinth that rests on three supports. It is a difficult site, open in two directions, and with an exacting architectonic background.

The 'Reclining Figure' now dominates the area in front of the building like a natural phenomenon, like a rock in the sea. Its surface is as though eroded by wind and wave. The carving has as many aspects as there are angles of vision and looks different from every viewpoint. If the spectator approaches it from the direction of the head, he is confronted by the mass of the limbs ending in a triangle; passing it on the right, he stands before the mighty, towering mountain of the right thigh, under which a tunnel has been bored. The upper part of the body rises steeply and majestically, as in the bronze of the Musée d'Art Moderne, Paris; the arms remain within the block, and the character of the block dominates the whole composition: the hollows and openings remain entirely subservient to the mass of stone. The body is no longer put down over the hollow space, but is "only the shell holding the hole. Recently I have tried to make the forms, and the spaces (not holes) inseparable, neither being more important than the other" (1953). This is most clearly evident when we approach the rear of the sculpture, the enormous opening, through which we perceive "the forms in recession inhabiting a tunnel" in the most various views and foreshortenings. The head, a Janus head, has been worked on both sides, with the back also modelled, and what is intended as hair assumes the shape of a face. The head rests upon the tall, columnar neck like a rocky crown on top of a cliff; this latest 'Reclining Figure' is royal, or rather divine, for it is the image of a deity, the incarnation of what Moore has always visualized as the oneness of man and earth, humanity and nature, spirit and intuition.

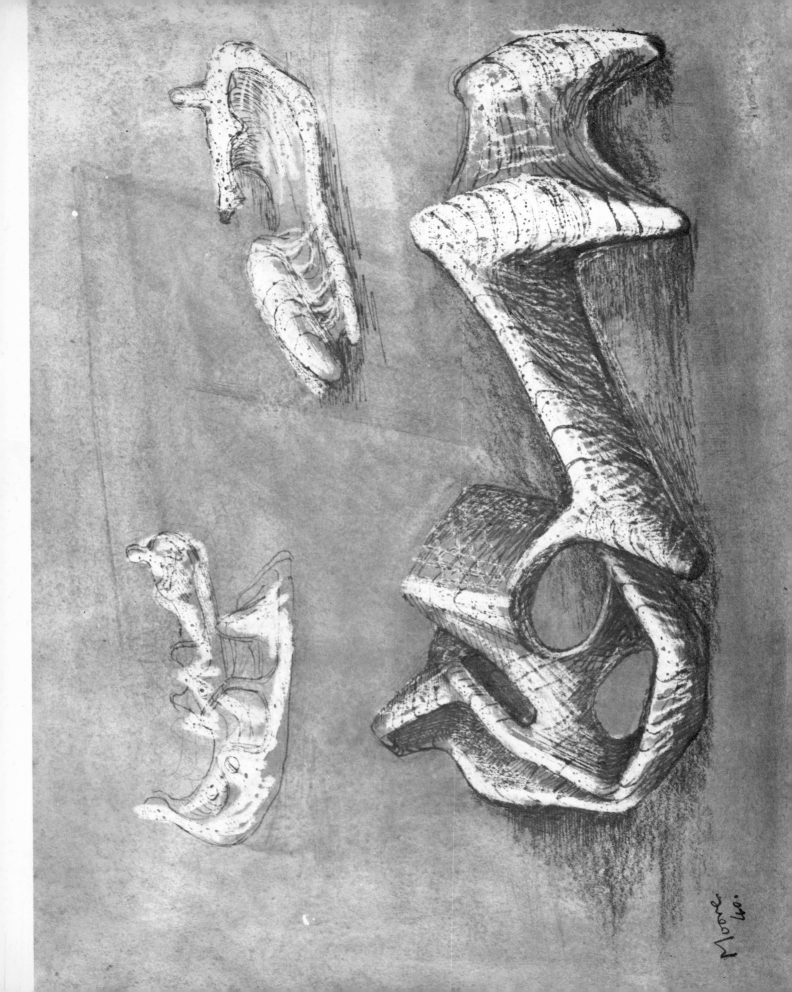

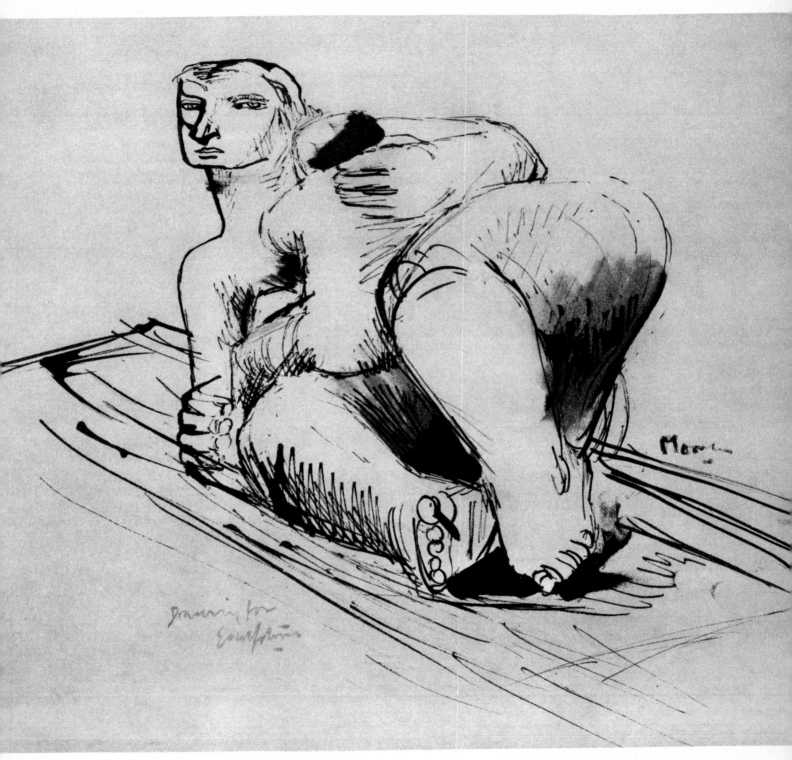

17

18

21

22

23

24

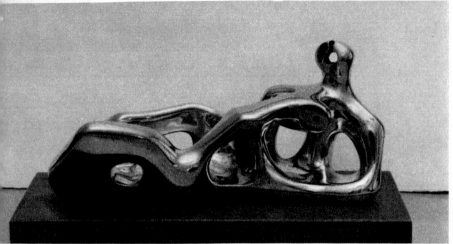

25

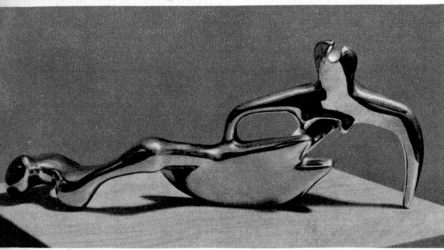

26

27

28

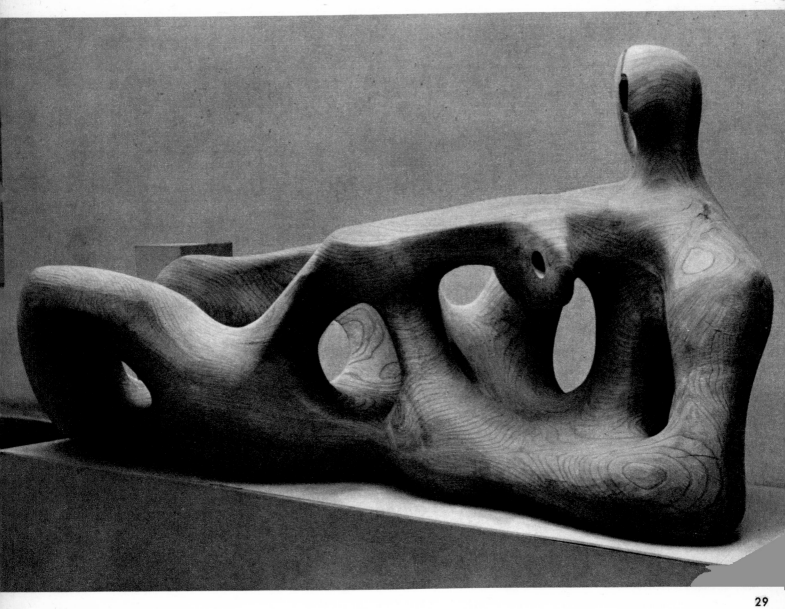

29

30

33
34

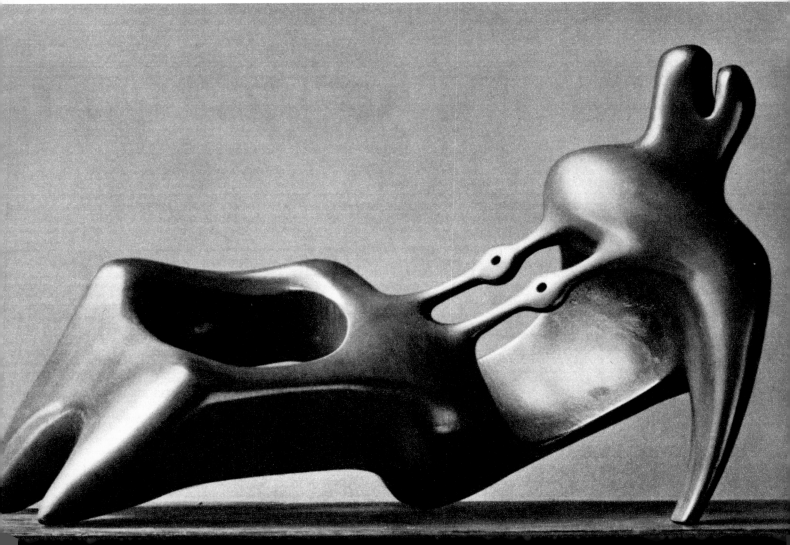

35

36

37

41

42

43

44

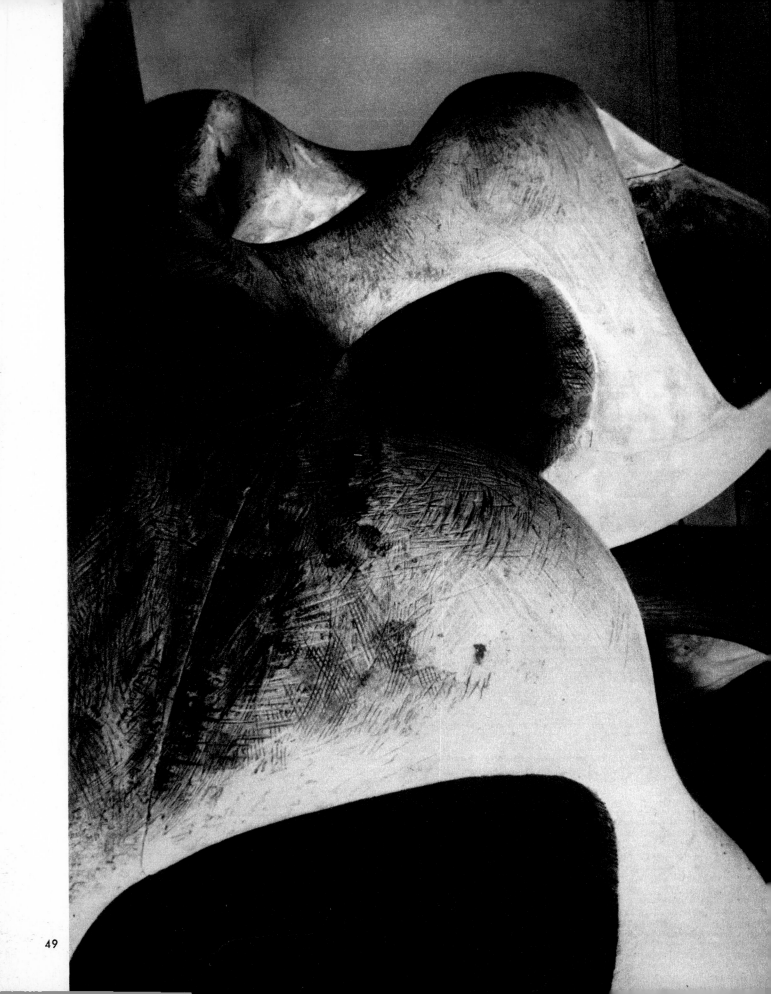

51

56

57

58

59

62

63

64

66

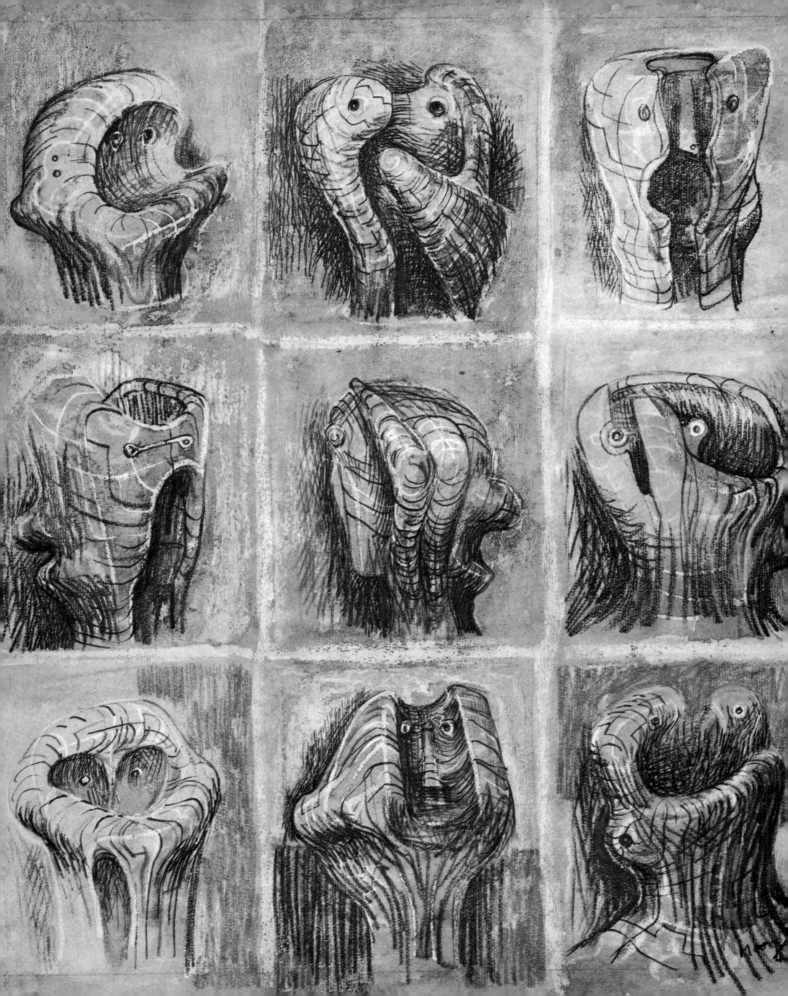

# THE ABSTRACT COMPOSITIONS
## AND THE 'STRING FIGURES'

As the fundamental theme of his work, the 'Reclining Figure' radiates out on to all areas of his creative labours; Moore's work is a totality and there are threads leading from one composition to the next, even though they are often hard to discern. Hence much can be learnt from observing the diversity and unity that mark the compositions that express Moore's basic character.

Moore is not an "abstract" artist; he is abstract in some of his works only by comparison with the more representational and symbolic ones. In the 1930s he was more of a Surrealist, without, however, identifying himself with the Surrealist movement. His works are most closely related to those of Jean Arp with their swelling organic forms, and the act of creation remains a primary force also in those works in which it is difficult to discern. In 1936 he took part in the International Surrealist Exhibition in London, and in 1937 in the exhibition of Fantastic Art at the Museum of Modern Art, New York. Nevertheless, human forms are present even behind the products of his fantasy, and Moore's fellow-exhibitors would undoubtedly have repudiated his words: "Although the non-logical, instinctive, subconscious part of the mind must play its part in his work, the artist also has a conscious mind which is not inactive. The artist works with a concentration of his whole personality, and the conscious part of it resolves conflicts, organizes memories, and prevents him from trying to walk in two directions at the same time ... All good art has contained both abstract and surrealist elements, just as it has contained both classical and romantic elements—order and surprise, intellect and imagination, conscious and unconscious" (1937).

When looking at Moore's abstract works, however, we must also recall another remark he made: "The sensitive observer of sculpture must learn to feel shape simply as shape." Not every piece of sculpture arouses a helpful association. The 'Two Forms' of 1934 (wood, Plate 70) or the wooden 'Form' of 1935 (Plate 74) appeal to our sympathy with shapes that follow an organic pattern and our feeling for wood that inspire an immediate desire to touch them with our hands. The 'Three Points' (1939, lead, Plate 75), on the other hand, threateningly command the observer to keep his distance. The 'Three Forms' of 1934 (stone, Plate 71) are built up of smaller shapes, a piece of prehistoric architecture that has a magical effect. That the 'Square Form' of 1936 (stone, Plate 72) recalls the head of an antediluvian monster or a Neanderthal man is quite irrespective of whether Moore's imagination tended in this direction or not. As Moore remarks: "There are universal shapes to which everybody is subconsciously conditioned and to which they can respond if their subcon-

scious control does not shut them off." The universal feelings aroused by these shapes constitute a link between the sculptor and the observer. Seeing such works as these at the opening of an exhibition in Athens, a Greek, Angelos Procopion, recalled the legend of Deucalion and Pyrrha. They repopulated the earth after the Flood by throwing down behind them stones which they had picked up and warmed. "Can one depict these stones at the moment of their amazing transformation?" he asked. "Can one depict the shapes a great block of stone will assume when it suddenly becomes warm, takes on life, begins to move, and here and there to swell? Moore's sculptural works are realizations of such a mythological vision."

The drawings and watercolours of these years now show the same character of form and expression. The sheet, from 1937, with the eleven ideas for sculpture (detail, colour plate page 31 and Plates 69 and 76) reveal how far Moore had ventured into the regions of free invention and with what great success. These "notes" are diagrams from memory and intuition. The watercolour (1935, colour plate page 21) shows that Moore occasionally advanced to the frontiers of the harmonic.

The 'String Figures' (1939, Plates 77—80) can be interpreted either as a vision, or, more probably a task Moore set himself. How can the tangible, the tactile be combined with the intangible, how wood or lead with threads, so as to give rise to a reality with a life of its own? How can space be delimited both inward and outward? The threads close and open, form an enclosed space and at the same time can be passed through towards the inside and towards the outside. We recall that, casting his mind back to his visits to the British Museum, Moore mentioned the 'bird-in-a-cage' carvings of New Ireland among the items of primitive art that made an impression upon him. One of Moore's 'String Figures' is actually called 'Bird Basket'; adding the idea of flight to that of bounded and unbounded space. There are also objects that look like heads, or like a tabernacle, or a mother and child, and one of them is called 'Bride'. The titles can be no more than metaphors, for the reality of the figures is new and not to be put into words. It would be a mistake to push association so far as to speak of a bridal veil of threads and so forth. The constructions are far too spiritual and have the same spectral existence, as, for example, the early surrealistic compositions of Giacometti. In certain drawings and watercolours of figures in space this affinity is even greater; here Moore comes closest to the spirit of Surrealism. In the 1950s he returns to these ideas in the sculptures placed in front of walls or within imaginary rooms.

## FIGURES, HEADS AND HELMETS

The compositions of the 1930s Moore referred to as figures or heads were no closer to nature than the 'String Figures'. The 'Compositions' in wood of 1932 and 1933 (Plates 81, 82) retain the greatest element of the human and organic, especially the second, though the first, with its handle, looks somewhat like an exotic jug. In his drawings Moore has repeatedly sought to effect an integration between a jug and a figure, and the two stone forms (1933, Plates 84, 85) have something of the ancient Mexican jug about them. The deeper the abstraction goes and the simpler it is, the more easily archaicisms make their appearance. Despite its small scale, the marble 'Figure' of 1937 (Plate 87) is as massive as an Easter Island idol. But most exciting is the 'Composition' in cement from 1932 (Plate 86). It had a jug shape, an eye, breasts — so it must be female, although the association of a bird, an owl for instance, is inescapable. There is something magical about the swelling shapes, the interpenetration of the volumes, the contrast between the thrusting forces and the perfection of sculptural form. The great eye is exorcism. Who can say whether the lead 'Figure' of 1940 (Plate 88) is also a standing figure? The perforation at the top might suggest a head, the lower part feet; then the projecting lobes would be the torso. Primitive it is, but modern technology is more pronounced.

Moore's 'Heads' are as surreal as his 'Figures'. The 1936 'Marble' (Plate 89) is a horizontal, lunar face looking upward, the details incised or slightly raised in low relief, rather as Ben Nicholson was doing at this time in his "painted reliefs." The 1937 'Head' (stone, Plate 90), although only 21 ins high, might well have the dimensions of a menhir or an Easter Island head it is so monumental. Moore would probably have adopted this scale if it would have been physically possible to carry out the sequence of his ideas. The perforations suggest eye and mouth, the engraved lines facial relationships. Moore also employs similar lines, which we know from ancient Babylonian oracle stones, in the 'Square Form' of 1946 and in some of his 'Reclining Figures' in order to convey messages that would otherwise have burst out of the sculptural framework.

In 1940 Moore made the first 'Helmet' (bronze, Plate 91, drawings, 1939 and 1944, colour plates pages 100, 109), which was followed by two more in 1950 and another two in 1952, making a total of six during this period if we include the 'Openwork Heads' among them. The coloured drawing outlines the problem, the sheet with heads from 1944 fills it in. The task of establishing concord between inner and outer shapes had already preoccupied Moore in some of the 'Reclining Figures' of the 1930s and in the 'String Figures'; the subject was to culminate in the 'Inner and Outer Forms' of 1951 to 1954. He calls the 1939 crayon drawing "heads for metal sculptures" and they prefigure the 'Helmets' of 1940. In two of the six small sketches a neck can be distinguished, enclosing the inner figure; in the others this is contained in a kind of foot. The figure looks out through the open helmet. Its two feelers (eyes) unite in four of the sketches and push the eyes back to the rear wall of the skull or helmet. If we compare the 1939 drawing with the 'Nine Heads' sketched in 1944, we see that the third head belongs to the 'Helmet' sequence; the rest lack the interior figure, though all but one are open. Henry Moore made numerous other drawings during the 1940s and 1950s that belong to the helmet-head series.

After the head, particularly in the bronzes dating from the late 1930s, had been reduced to something like a knob or a saddle, it returned to a position of central importance around 1940, the year of the drawings in London air raid shelters. The possibility that steel helmets and gas masks, the paraphernalia of war and defence, played a motivating role cannot be dismissed out of hand, but in Moore's case this factor can only have served as a confirmation of his inner ideas.

The helmet as a protective covering is in line with his sculptural imagery for the opening in the helmet reflects his experiments with transparency; only the figure inside is new and all the more moving because of its human appearance. The psychologist speaks of child or soul, an interpretation that seems immediately probable because Moore had visualized a content of this or a similar nature since the beginning. In a 'Mother and Child' (1928) he places the child so deep in the mother's lap that it already gives the observer a feeling of inside-being. To give shape to the invisible as well as the visible has always been one of the artist's tasks, and Moore is equally determined to include the psychological element in his work. "The meaning and significance of form probably depends on the countless associations of man's history" (1937). The concept of "man's history" is an idea of the soul which is one of those psychological archaicisms that permeates Moore's work. Its current modification lies in its combination with the helmet.

The concept of the inner figure of 1940 changes in the 'Helmets' of 1950 (Plates 92—94) into a more compact shape, that has something repellent, technological and warlike about it that is not unlike a stereo-telescope. Mythological abstract conceptions always have many meanings, and the combination of images from the primeval levels of the mind with topical actuality is not unusual. During the air attacks on London, Moore's thoughts must have circled round life and death that subsequently led to compositions such as these. The helmet and internal shapes of 1950 are, in any case, frightening, combative, as compositions not far removed from representations of death. There is a remarkable sketch for a lithograph from 1939 showing a face behind a cagelike mask, or barbed wire (owned by Irina Moore). This sketch may be a wartime experience and stand on its own or may already contain the idea of the

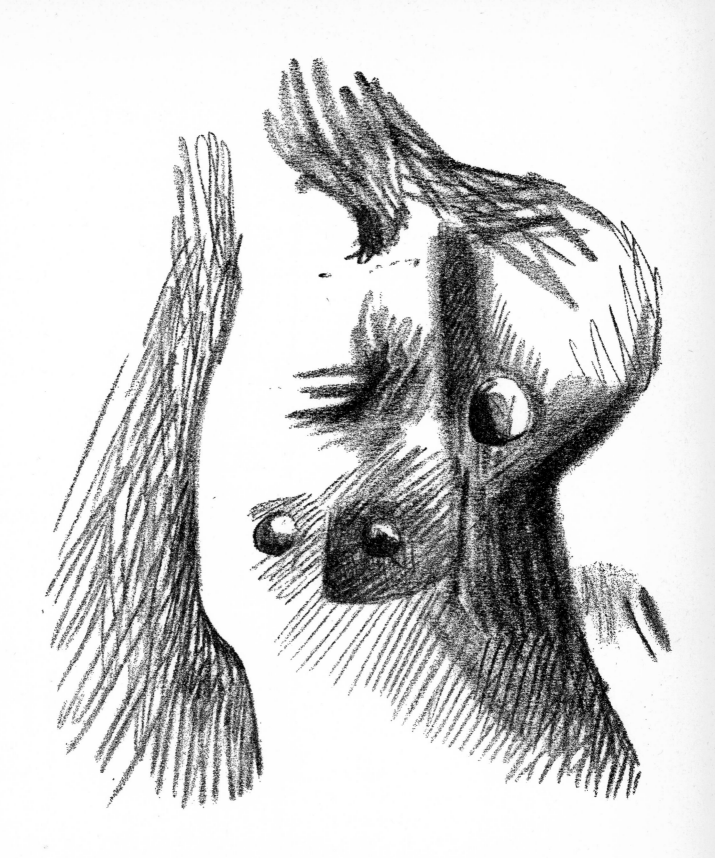

'Helmet' and the ensuing 'Openwork Heads' that gradually have evolved. This would mean that the interior figure started its journey in the present and then travelled back into the mythological past.

The 1950 'Openwork Heads' (bronze, Plates 95—97) are lighter, more amiable, more womanly. The plaited strips, which, like open lattice-work, form the back of the head (hair) and the shoulders, are modelled with extreme refinement in wax and cast "à cire perdue". The heads are hollow; eye, nose and mouth incised or painted on. Their warlike flavour, the idea of armour and knighthood, vizor and helmet, is not to be explained by the shape alone. Underlying them may also be additional associations from memory, from British history, the Norman Invasion, from literature and from the medieval sculpture on cathedrals and town halls Moore saw as a child. They do not refer to the 'hollow man' of the inter-war years; the arabesque nature of the forms tends in the opposite direction, the mysterious grace of the disguise is a sublimation of wartime experiences, their transference to a poetic plane, such as that of Shakespeare's historical plays.

During these years Moore also produced some lifelike heads, such as the one of 1953 in the antique style or the portrait-like 'Small Head' (1953, bronze, Plate 99), secondary works that show Moore from an unproblematical angle, as a sculptor of great representational ability. Of greater importance are the 'Animal Heads' from 1952 to 1956: the 'Goat's Head' (1952, bronze, Plate 100), and the tragic head of a mythological creature (1951, bronze, Plate 102) and the chimera-like head of 1956 (bronze, Plate 103). In these are poignant metaphors. Moore's pantheism incorporates the animals into the world of his creative imagination and transforms them on this plane into a pantragism. A page of animals' heads dating from 1954 (Plate 101) shows nine studies of fabulous beasts, as forceful in expression as in their purely graphic qualities.

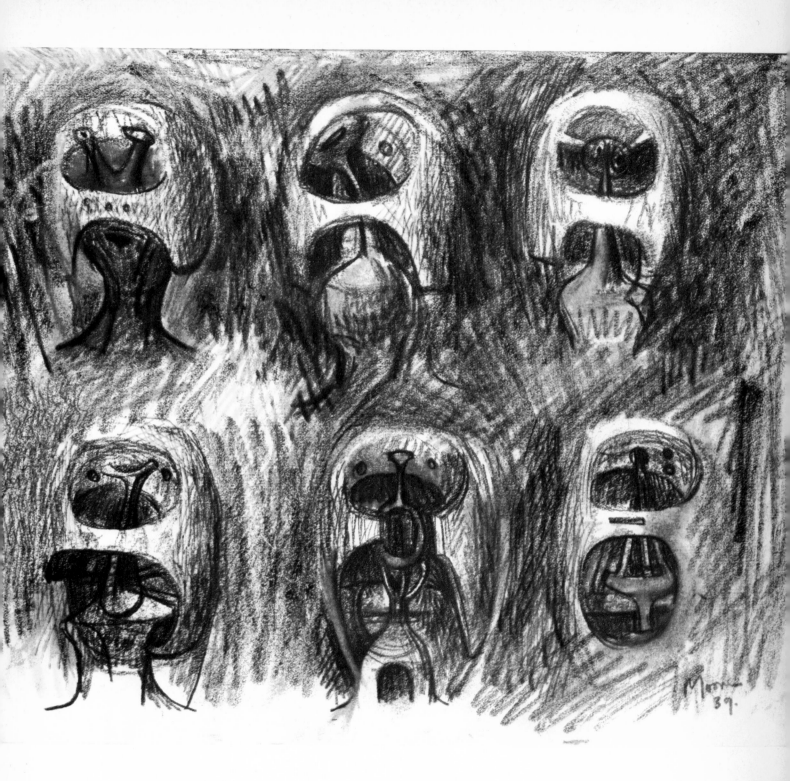

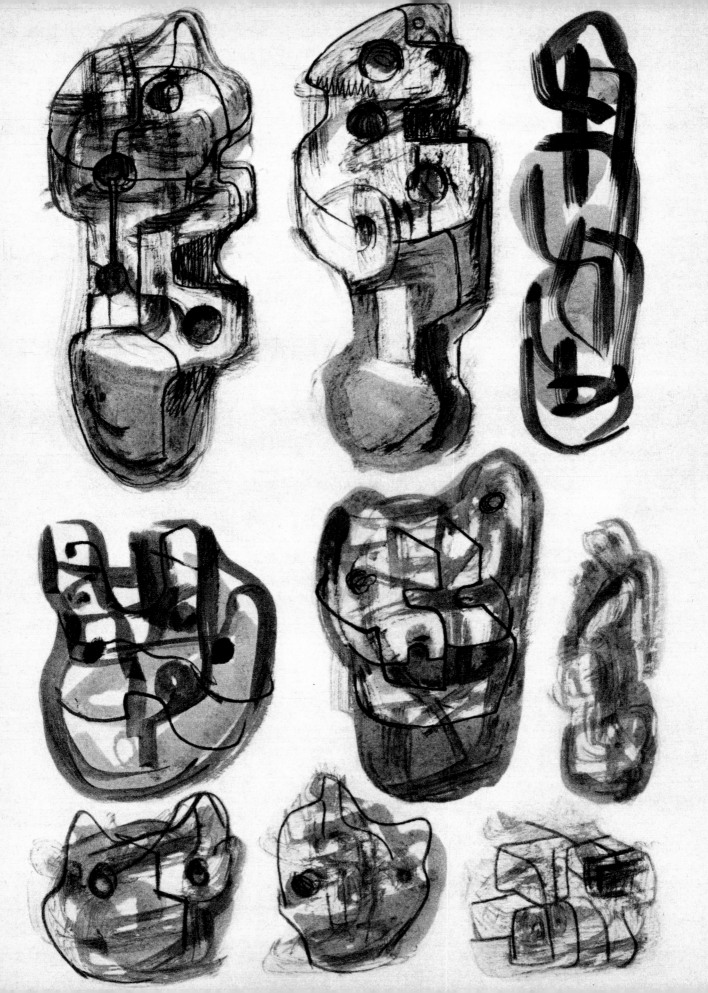

73

4

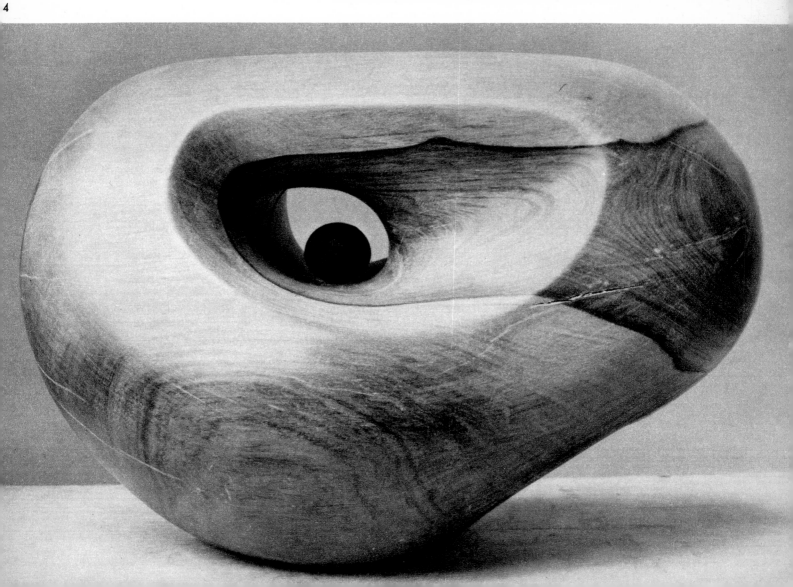

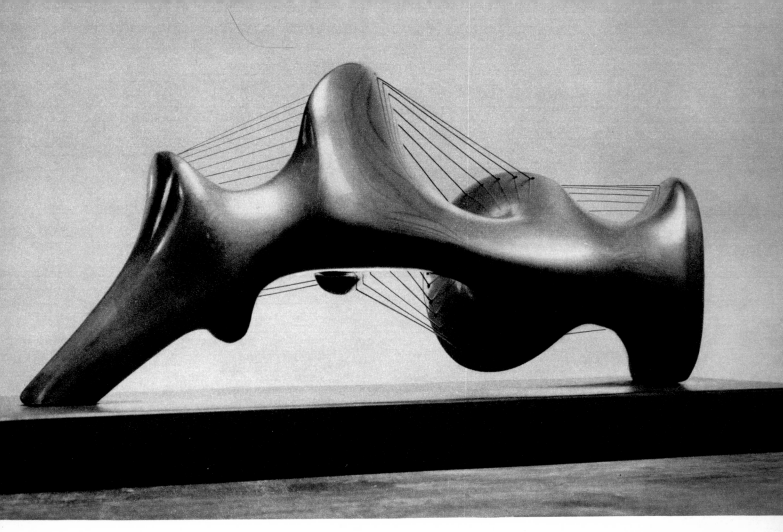

77

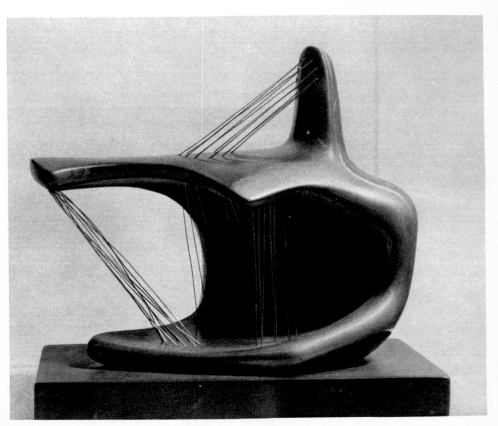

78

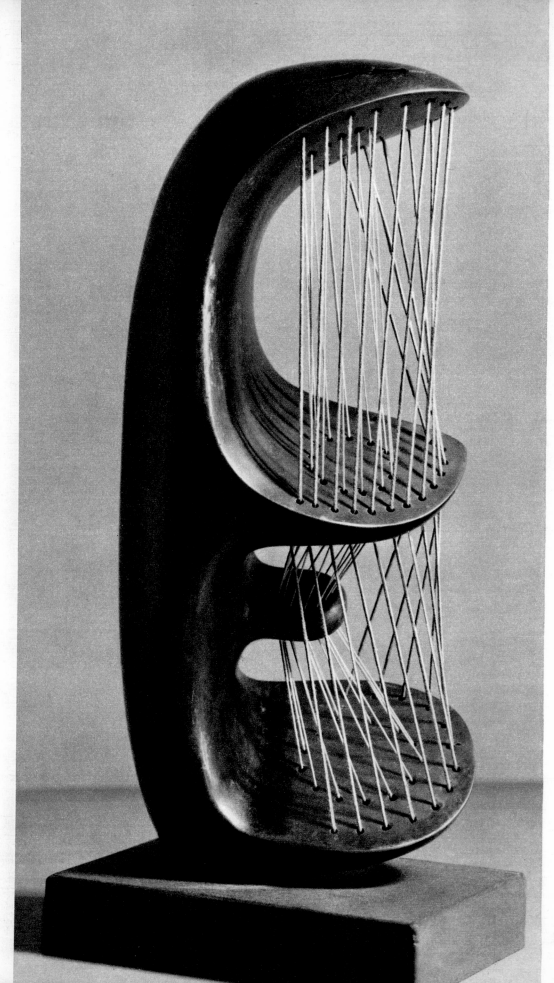

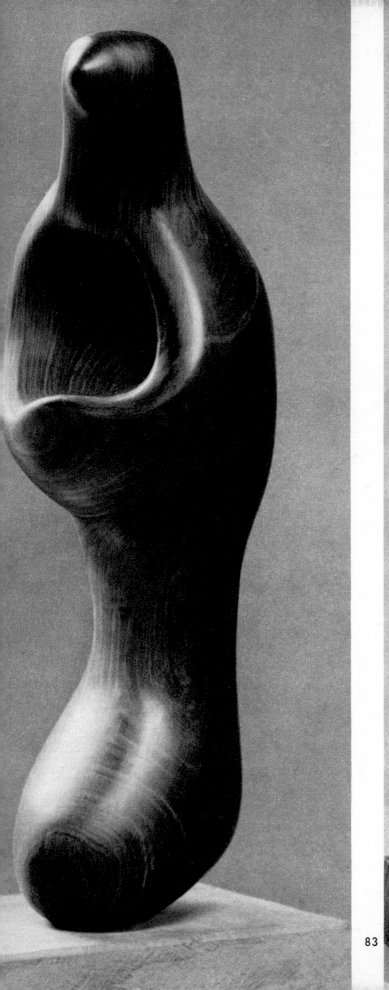

84

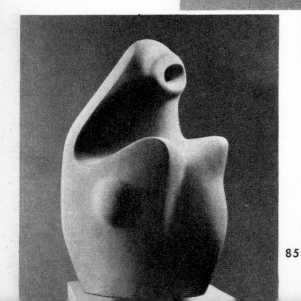

85

86

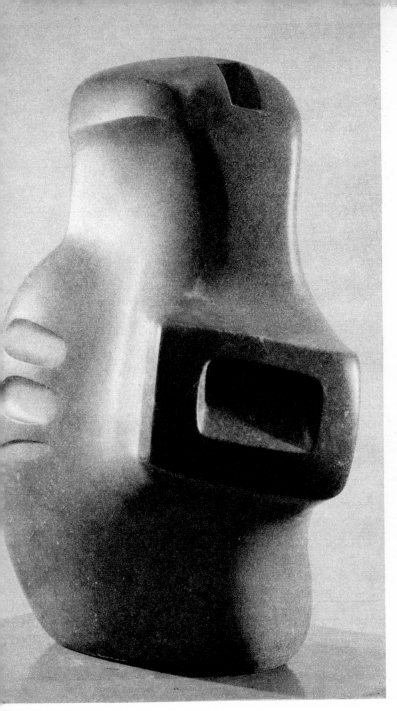

87                                    88

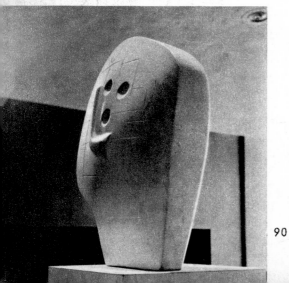

90

91

94

95

96

97

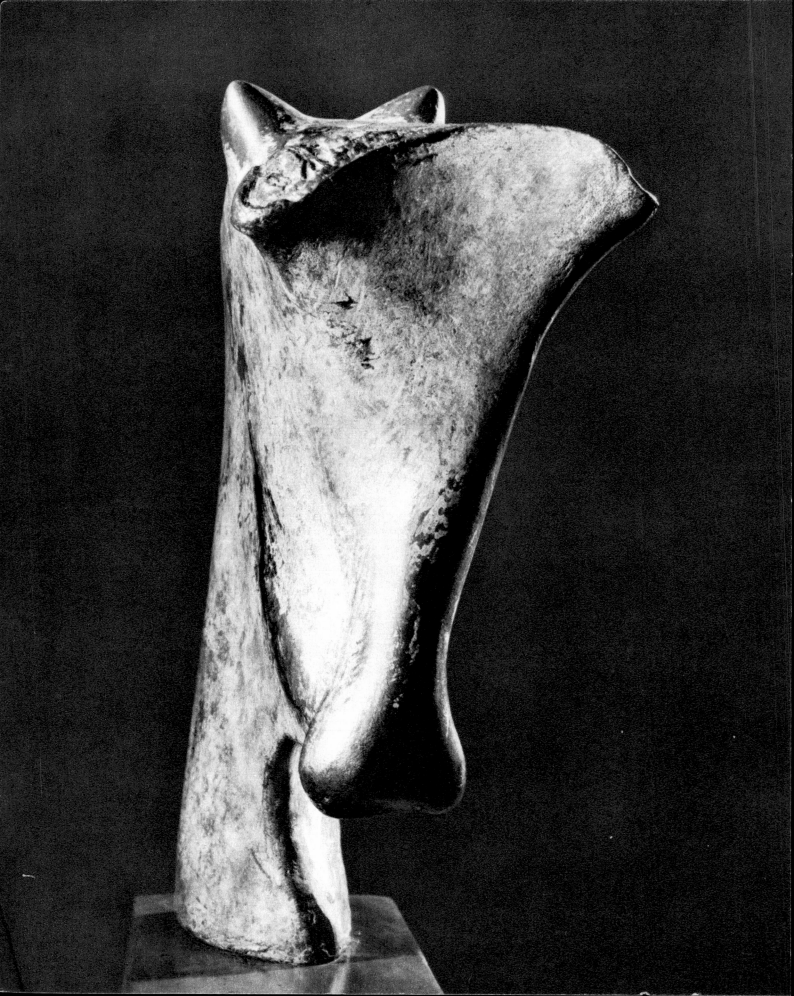

fabulous animals.

102

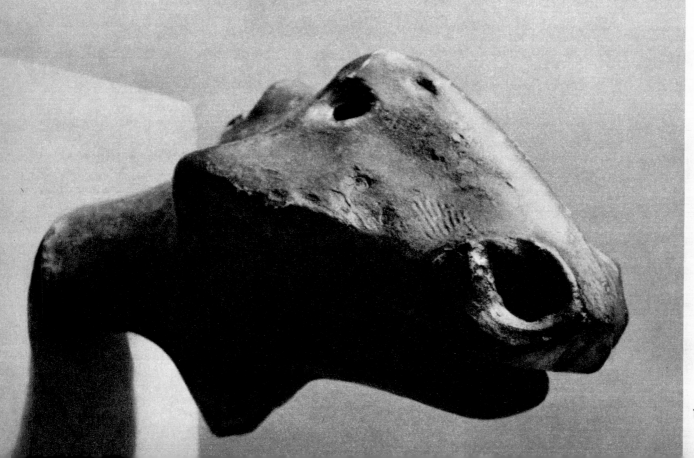

103

## SHELTER DRAWINGS. NORTHAMPTON MADONNA
## FAMILY GROUPS. MOTHER AND CHILD

The theme 'Mother and Child' preoccupied Moore from the outset, and up to 1930 it followed a course parallel with that of other subjects. Since there are two figures in a relation to each other, the group will have a certain duality, a dialogue of one figure with another. But in the early versions this tendency is less important than the feeling for the stone as a single block, a unified mass. In 1936 he produced a stone carving that has the muteness of Bronze Age megalithic monuments, and in 1938 and 1939 he created three versions on the lines of the 'String Figures'. The emotional values are not separated from the sculptural means and the object is not conceived on traditional lines. The 'Mother and Child', like the 'Reclining Figure', is an expression of Moore's belief in nature and fruitfulness.

The theme remained in the background for some years, until two events brought it to the fore again: the commission to draw the occupants of London's air raid shelters, and the commission from Canon Rowden Hussey, Vicar of St Matthew's, Northampton, to carve a 'Madonna and Child' for his church, the same church for which Graham Sutherland was to paint a 'Crucifixion' and Benjamin Britten to write a Festival Cantata.

The shelter drawings have become Moore's most popular and most frequently reproduced works. The community of experience shared by all those affected by the war, and the directness of portrayal, made these drawings universally understood. Moore saw his own theme, the 'Reclining Figure', embodied in every human and formal variation. The cavern, the protective bowels of the earth, the protective cloak of the mother, the rugs and blankets that at one moment seemed to be a warm covering, at another a shroud, all this was familiar to Moore and moved him deeply as something with which he was most intimately concerned. There are countless wrappings, stretching out in endless rows, at bottomless depths; human destinies assume typical expressive shapes, fixed postures, and it is always women he draws, reclining, or more rarely seated women, mothers with their children, and where the women have children they automatically assume the stature of Madonnas through the immensity of their responsibility (Plate 108). These drawings prefigure the commission for St Matthew's.

As drawings, the shelter pages differ greatly in composition and technique. There are sleeping women of a realism that recalls Pieter Bruegel the Elder, with open mouths and lifeless masks (plate 106), sprawling figures of whose creaturely existence nothing is left but a bundle of straw, which Moore portrays with a bundle of dry strokes. But in the hours of terror there is also the sublimity and grandeur of women

who sit there in imperturbable dignity and women who watch over destiny like Fates. Moore has transmitted them to posterity and called one of the drawings 'Three Fates'. Technically the drawings are executed with great care and perfection. Moore uses pencil and chalk, brush and pen, coloured inks and watercolours, and combines the media in accordance with the subject; sombre drawings with a basis of dark chalk alternate with strongly lit and aggressively colourful ones; the whole gamut of his feelings and discoveries is mirrored in the colour-range.

The following year Moore continued his work as official war artist in the coal mines, drawing the miners at work underground. This series is little known, although it cannot fail to interest everyone concerned with Moore, because here the sculptor, for the first time, dealt with the theme of the man, and because he did not approach it from outside, being himself a miner's son. It does not look, however, as though he found himself again in this region of his youth. Moore understood by caverns something other than pit shafts, and the theme was less rewarding for him (Plate 104). Work on the Northampton 'Madonna' began in 1943. The first phase was a number of drawings and a few models, of which two were cast in bronze. The first is no more than a mother and child, the second (Plate 109) is already a religious image.

The last decades have shown that valid religious art still can be created on the basis of genuine Christian feeling and contemporary design. The most convincing examples have been produced for Catholic Churches in France (Assy, Vence, Audincourt); the Protestant and Anglican Churches have been less creative. Moore received the commission from the church as a man and an artist, not as a member of a religious communion. Could his work be religious? The result provides an affirmative answer to this question; the 'Madonna' is profoundly religious and worthy of the sculptor, although he sacrificed his freedom to the idea embodied in the task and, as with the commission for the shelter drawings, adopted an 'outward attitude'. It was clear to him that the 'Madonna' could not be simply a 'Mother and Child', but he believed that he could evolve a Madonna out of this theme, if he lent it "an austerity and a nobility, and some touch of grandeur (even hieratic aloofness) ... a quiet dignity and gentleness". He finally executed the commission in the years 1943 and 1944 (stone, St Matthew's Church, Northampton, Plates 110—111).

This work displays the qualities of all Moore's sculpture. As in the 'Reclining Figure' and the 'Time and Life' terrace, the folds are drawn taut over a frame that thrusts out from within, and the looser sections of drapery fulfil a similar function, except that the hard stone does not leave the sculptor the freedom of bronze. That Moore chose stone shows how seriously he took the commission and how much he wished to give the divine mother a look of calm and simplicity, the appearance of being fixed in her pose to all eternity. The axes are slightly displaced by the angle of her head and

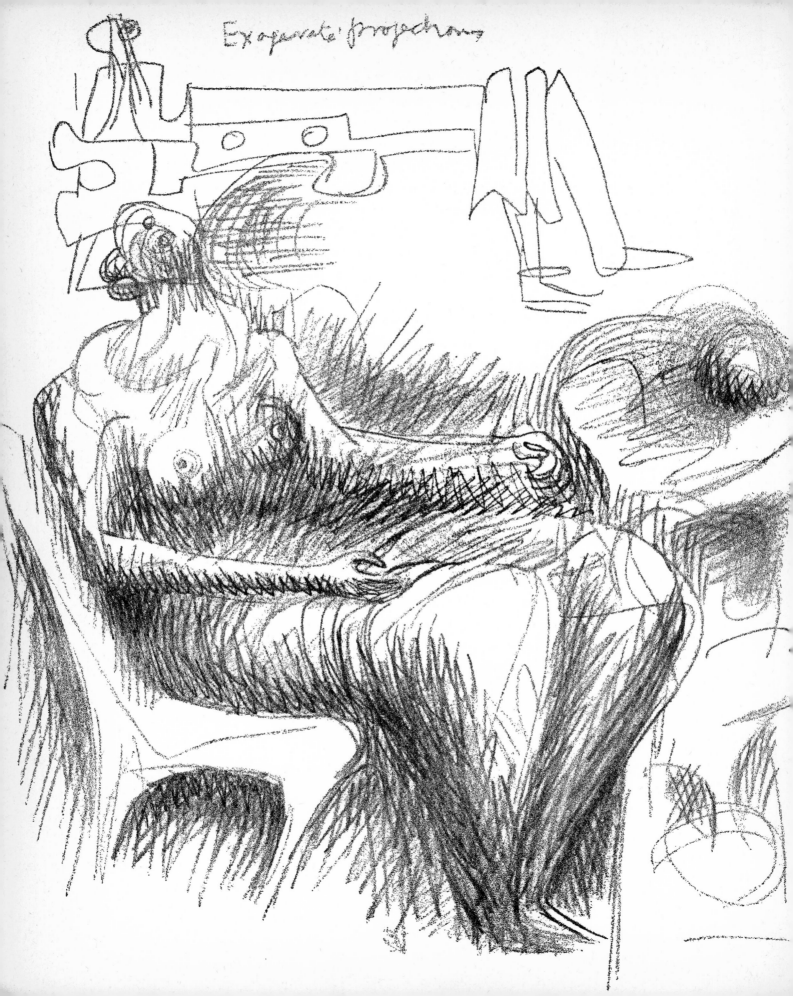

Exaperate *projections*

diagonal of the Child's legs, the skulls are almost spherical, the modelling of faces and drapery is restrained. Similarity to any ecclesiastical style, such as the Romanesque, which is so close to the sculptor, has been avoided.

The 'Madonna' has the same sincerity and integrity as the rest of Moore's works, even though it does not come from the same depth of the unconscious nor possess quite the same imaginative power. In this respect, it stands closest to the 'Memorial Figure' at Dartington Hall for what there creates a classical effect, here produces a religious one. It is in keeping with Moore's principles, however, to exert all his energy on a commission that automatically imposed restrictions upon him from the outset. The problems involved related less to art than to society, which, contrary to earlier generations down to the baroque, does not so much demand that the artist bow to its worldly or spiritual dogmas, as that shall submit to its artistic judgment. In exceptional instances, a contemporary religious work can ignore the congregation, as at Assy; or else it can remain on their level, as Moore's does. "I do not really want to play the role of the obvious disturber. The bogy-man business I leave . . . to others," he wrote in 1957. He is always concerned with art, never with a dubious up-to-dateness.

With the 'Family Group' theme Moore regained his freedom since the commissions he received were less restricting. He started work on these groups at about the same time as the 'Madonna'. In the years 1944 to 1947 he produced a number of larger and smaller variations in stone, bronze and terracotta, differing considerably from one another, being both naturalistic and non-naturalistic, though never as 'abstract' as the 'Reclining Figures'. The theme does not hem him in, but it demands a certain readiness to enter into the meaning of a community such as the family. "To be an artist is to believe in life," Moore writes, and this includes community life.

According to Herbert Read, Moore made fourteen preparatory clay models between the autumn of 1944 and the spring of 1945, of which the first served as a basis for the 'Family Group' in stone that today stands in Harlow New Town while he employed the remainder for seven bronzes, one of which is now in the Tate Gallery, London. Moreover, four smaller ones followed by 1947.

The small bronze of 1944 (Plate 120) is among those closest to nature and more gentle. The parents sit lightly and close together, the man's right hand rests on the woman's right shoulder, and the child, leaning forward, sits easily on his mother's thigh. In gesture, a curved, slightly baroque movement runs through the group as a whole. The later bronze group (Plate 122), by contrast, is strictly and consciously composed and devoid of individual parts. The arms are fused into a semicircle surrounding the two children. There are round, flowing rhythms in the upper zone, pointed in the lower. The group of the parents with two children, one standing and one sitting (1946, Plate 121)), similarly, is closed and non-naturalistic; Moore executed it in bronze and in terracotta; in the bronze version it looks tender and soft, in the terracotta hard and rough. Since the artist usually works the surface after casting, he is able to vary the expressions of the different examples of one and the same composition considerably.

This 'Family Group' is rather far removed from the others in its formal aspects. The man's chest is an open hollow as in the 'Reclining Figures' in Buffalo and Wakefield; the woman's right breast is negatively modelled, the left positively; the legs are as rigid as the string-boards of a church pew. The boy standing between his father's knees is statuesquely simplified, the child sitting on his mother's lap is reaching with his left hand for her open breast, but the hand is lost in the bulk of the mother's body. The expression of the group is archaic, mute; the human relationship between the four beings is expressed only through the convergent attitude of the figures and through the alternations of solid shapes and hollows. The woman's hollow is fruitfulness, the man's is spirit. His figure would culminate less consciously in the raised head, if the shoulders did not sit like the arch of a bridge over the broad opening of the chest. An indication of the position of the man in Moore's œuvre: he stands outside its centre, and when he does become part of it, it is as head of the family, king or warrior.

The bronze group of 1946 (Plate 123, Museum of Modern Art, New York) goes a step further. The chest of both parents is concave, the man's head cloven, and there is something tragic, protesting, challenging about this cleavage. All life is conflict in Moore's view: art and life are made up of conflicts. But as always, Moore does not cling to this solution; in an exceedingly expressive group for the Barclay School, Stevenage (bronze, 1945—9, Plates 124, 125), he returns to naturalism. Is this out of consideration for the site? A cloven head is certainly not likely to be understood on a school playground, but of more decisive significance is the fact that Moore sees greater or less naturalism as purely a question of degree, not as an antithesis. The direct and the indirect may very well be coeval and supplement one another. Looking through the drawings, we find one of the most abstract treatments right at the beginning of the series (1944)—the sketch for a bronze, cast in 1947, for the National Gallery of Melbourne.

The 'Family Groups' are followed in time by the 'Rocking Chair'. From 1950 to 1952 Moore produced six pieces of a mother and child in a rocking chair with or without a ladderlike back. They are enchanting impromptus, the offspring of a lighter muse. One is inclined to suppose that family life underwent a happy release of tension through his young daughter Mary, forgetting that at the same period the frightful 'Helmet' series came into being. To the artist's many-sided consciousness there cor-

142

responds a pluralism of his conceptions and their varying depths. As with Mozart, tragedy is next door to comedy, and happy works are not born out of easier situations and vice versa; jubilation is more genuine when behind it stands the totality of life with all its "unresolved conflicts". The 'Rocking Chair' first appears in a drawing of 1948 (Plate 112) of the mother with the two-year-old Mary. The three versions of 1950 are likewise full of grace, but by 1952 this theme, too, assumes a mythological character: the heads become archaic knots, the bodies clothed skeletons, but the expression remains elated (Plate 114). A reversal takes place in 'Mother and Child' (1952/3, bronze, Plate 115); the two concavely modelled beings sit facing one another on a Delphic tripod like birds of prey, forced into a semicircular unity. They are harpies like those on an antique monument in the British Museum. The child is seeking with its bird's beak for its mother's breast, although it cannot drink but only wound; the jagged comb of the mother's face is deadly, not even human, let alone motherly; the theme turns into its opposite, the human or divine into the diabolical.

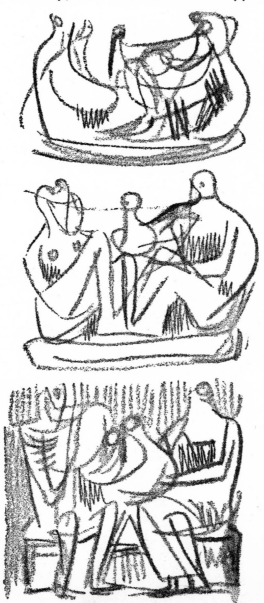

The theme crops up once more in its original form in 1956 and 1957, in 'Mother and Child with Apple' (bronze, 1956, Plates 116, 117) and 'Mother and Child in front of an open wall' (1957, bronze, Plates 118, 119). Both compositions are intimate: that with the apple combines the most contradictory elements into a superior unity, the primitive with the refinements of Donatello; the group in front of the wall, on the other hand, belongs to the sphere of ideas with which Moore wrestled when he sought a solution to the UNESCO commission: life, family, education. This composition must have offered itself to him, like the woman seated in front of a wall of the same period, as one of the possible variations on the theme.

143

## THE 'THREE STANDING FIGURES'
## IN BATTERSEA PARK

The years of the 'Family Groups' saw the production of a group of three figures that has been looked upon as having an affinity with them and has also been interpreted as father, mother and daughter. The figures do have something of the family about them, but the hieratic element predominates (1947/8, stone, Plates 129—132). A first model was made in 1945/6 in terracotta, the second in bronze. In spite of its smallness, the terracotta model looks both monumental and mobile; the modelling is sketchy, but completely to the point, and the casualness of the detail bears the stamp of genius. The figures stand side by side as though by chance, in easy attitudes, and yet nothing in them could be changed. The drawing belonging to this model (Plate 128) differs from it so greatly that it is almost a separate composition in its own right. Moore must have worked on the composition for a long time, before he arrived at this trinity. According to the 1940 drawings, we must assume that these are Fates, divine beings who, in Classical mythology, have power even over the gods. There is an obvious temptation to identify them, the left-hand one as Clotho, who spins the thread of life, the middle one as Lachesis, who receives it, and the right-hand, one-eyed figure as Atropos, who severs it. Among the Romans Clotho was called Parca or Fata and was first the goddess of birth, before becoming the goddess of fate, a combination of fate and birth that is also in line with Moore's ideas.

The left-hand figure is unquestionably the most human and naturalistic, her face is visible, while the other two wear a veil that leaves only the upper part of the face uncovered. Her garment hangs loosely from her shoulders and falls in unobtrusive folds over her abdomen and knees, her arms hang limp. The way in which the drapery is swathed round the hips of the other two gives them a more obtrusively costumed appearance, while their arms are held in more conscious poses. All three have something of the prophetess about them: they gaze into infinite distance, without betraying either boon or bane in their facial expression. They stand above things, are beings of a human kind, but not of this world, mysterious creatures, "neither frightful nor deadly in their magnificence", neutral creatures and strangely ambivalent in appearance.

Do they look Norse or Greek? Here, too, many interpretations are possible. The gloomy gaze of terracotta model suggests Norns, and Moore, as an Englishman, may have read Ossian before he came to Homer. There is as much of the Celtic spirit of Ireland and England in the veiled faces as there is of the Greek in the postures and drapery. Again and again we come in Moore's work upon something that stands above opposites, both formally and spiritually. This is disturbing, but the disturbing forms part of Moore's outlook on life. "All that is bursting with energy is disturbing," but this is accompanied by the sentence: "One must try to find a synthesis, to come to terms with opposite qualities" (1957). Do we here have a synthesis? In so far as the Fates do not merely contain, but also integrate, the antithetical elements previously noted in his make-up—the psychologically archaic and the conscious, nature and law, organic and abstract—we can speak of synthesis. It seems as though Moore had achieved this unity by means of "universal shapes to which everybody is subconsciously conditioned", shapes that remain valid through the ages and are contained both in the real and in the abstract.

## KING AND QUEEN

The human values of the 'Family Groups' and the supernatural pose of the Fates were followed by the mythological pair of a king and queen (1952/3, bronze, Plates 133—136). This work has been connected with the British Royal couple, because it was produced at the time of Elizabeth II's coronation, but Moore did not have this in mind. If there was any outside stimulus it came from the fact that he used to read stories about kings and queens to his little daughter—or so he says in his foreword to the catalogue of an exhibition in New York. At the same time, he points out that the key to the group is perhaps to be found in the king's head, that head and crown, face and beard are one and have something Pan-like, something almost animal and yet royal about them (we think involuntarily of the 1952 'Goat's Head', which is more than an animal's head). There is something mythological about the group, but to see references to Egyptian royal groups, such as the 18th-dynasty group in the British Museum, is incorrect; Moore could only have learnt from them what he did not want to do. There is nothing imperious about this royal pair; on the contrary, it is a very human couple, overbred and frail, that appears lost and lonely on the Scottish Highlands at Shawhead, Dumfries, looking out across a loch to the mountains. And yet mythological? The mythological element does not depend upon reference to some concrete datum from ancient times, the archaic Greek female figures, say, that are "grand and full like Handel's music", but upon the fact that it springs from a psychological constitution which, in the most natural way, combines the present with the beginnings. The "universal shapes" are shapes fundamental to the human soul and spirit, and they guide the sculptor's hand.

There are no preliminary studies, apart from a few drawings of 1951, which might belong to this theme, and two bronzes for the queen, one unclothed and with an arabesque head, the other resembling the final version, but without the diadem in the hair.

The two figures, in tranparent drapery, sit on a simple bench, without touching one another, the queen with hands folded in her lap, the king resting his arm on the bench. The torsos are flat and thin like ribbons, the backs concave. The surfaces are roughened—Moore now attaches great importance to working the surfaces in order to remove the tiresome smoothness of bronze, which causes the light to slide off too quickly, instead of allowing it time to bore its way in. The patient hands are filed down to the last detail, the arms and legs are slender, but the feet are firmly planted on the plinth as though they wished never to part from it. The garment of each figure falls down over the knees and hangs like an antependium in front of the group and the bench. The heads are fitted together as though out of standardized units;

the queen's emphasizes the vertical, thrusting against the diagonal coiffure surmounted by the semicircular diadem or crown. The king's head with the eye pierced through it only becomes a crown when seen within the context of the whole composition; the semicircular hoop (the crown itself) begins directly above the eyes and turns the head into a strange, animal-like object such as we find in ancient oriental and Egyptian deities. Moore says "Pan" and means the time when the animal predominated in gods. But Pan also means All, and Moore may also have thought of the combination of nature, man and animal, of the totality of the world, sculpturally speaking of the unity of natural and supernatural, objective and abstract. Thus there is synthesis here too, synthesis in the combination of the archaic with the contemporary, the unconscious with the spiritual. This is a highwater mark in Moore's creative work, a monument—for that is what it is—timeless and without specific purpose. It quickly won public recognition and higher esteem than the more naturalistic Madonnas at Northampton and for St Peter's Church in Claydon (1943 and 1949, stone). The effect of a contemporary work of art is as unpredictable as that of a problematic, but powerful contemporary personality. When they reach a certain degree of anonymity, works of art break free from their author and become subjects instead of objects. As such, they lead their own life and through it change their environment.

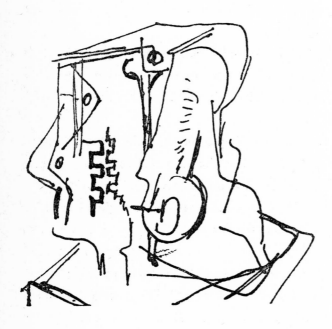

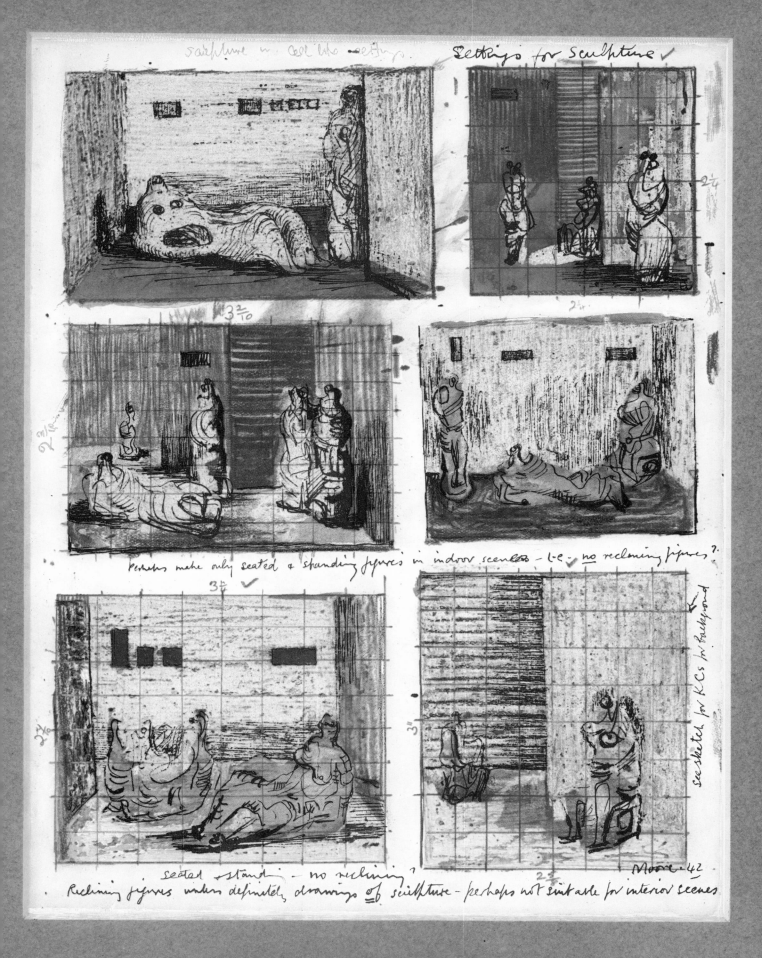

sculpture in cell like setting.                    Settings for Sculpture ✓

3²/10

Perhaps make only seated & standing figures in indoor scenes - i.e. - no reclining figures?

3⊞ ✓

seated + standing - no reclining?

Reclining figures makes definitely drawings of sculpture - perhaps not suitable for interior scenes

Moore -42

105

106

109

119

124

125

126

131

# SCULPTURE ON BUILDINGS

In 1952, while Moore was working on his 'Reclining Figure' for the 'Time and Life' building, the architect Michael Rosenauer suggested that he should design a screening wall to terminate the terrace at its Bond Street end. The suggestion, which developed into a commission, interested Moore especially since it afforded him for the first time an opportunity of working out, in conjunction with the architect, a design within an architectural project that was not yet completed in all its details. The sculpture was to be an integral part of the structure, not a "stuck-on-stone plaque" (Moore).

The most exciting thing for Moore was the fact that the balustrade was open on both sides, to the terrace and the street; hence he could work the stone from every side; he even thought of making the sculptures rotate, so that different sides would be visible at different times. This was unfortunately impossible for technical reasons: the individual pieces were too big and too heavy. We can see from the three-foot bronze model (1952, Plate 138) how Moore visualized the mobility of the fully three-dimensional parts: with a turn of 90 degrees the observer would look straight up at them from the street, and the short sides of the blocks would appear just as much shaped as the long sides.

Moore has himself described the evolution of the work (1954). He made four models. In the first he was disturbed by the repetition of the row of windows, in the second the vertical element seemed to him too pronounced, in the third, which stressed the horizontal, the uniform size of the parts struck him as unsatisfactory but the fourth, with a few modifications, he finally carried out. In the course of the work he introduced further improvements: for example he enlarged the openings, in order to give more individual life to the parts, of which in the end there were four.

The task was enormous, for the stone screening wall was 26 feet long and 10 feet high (1952/3, Portland stone, Plates 137, 139). Most of the work was done out of doors at Much Hadham, where Moore first rough-hewed the blocks with the help of a few young sculptors, before completing the final carving on his own.

The aim was not figurative carving in the true sense; its integration into the building suggested forms that might be one thing or another, but were firstly broadly carved blocks of stone that asserted themselves in relation to the building, not differentiated sculptures whose qualities only become effective at close quarters. The second block from the right looks as though it might be a large head and a squat body and does so even more distinctly when rotated; the second from the left is a genuine half-length figure with normal proportions when rotated, though when seen from the front it is an abstract framework. The two outer compositions gaze at one another, the grooves creating the impression of profiles, the lower halves functioning as

183

massive bases. We are reminded of Moore's predilection for Mexican art, during the late 1920s when he was working on the 'Reclining Figures', but the angularity of the shapes in the screening wall is distinct and new.

Of all his works, these carvings are closest to the abstractions of the 1930s, the primitive 'Mother and Child' of 1936, the 'Square Form' of 1936 (Plate 72) and the 'Figure' of 1937 (Plate 87). At that time, however, the block remained closed and not pierced; now Moore combines the block-like with the open; the experience of fifteen years lies behind him. It is impossible to reduce the whole work to a common denominator and side by side there are angular shapes and round ones, cubic blocks and bulging shapes, geometrical 'prefabricated units' and shapes that are organic and living. Changes in expression also arise from the fact that Moore penetrates deep into the tone, so that a great deal of play is allowed to light and shade in the total composition.

Although the carvings are integrated into the building, each can stand on its own. This was most clearly evident while Moore was still working on them at Much Hadham and the architectonic framework was absent. One could walk round them, look at them from all sides and observe that they were worked from every aspect, but with the emphasis on the front and the rear.

There are not many such sculptures on buildings; for the most part the client or architect is content to set up a piece of sculpture in a way that creates a focal point advantageous to the building. Perhaps it was due to the success of this undertaking that Moore received a further commission, the design of a long brick wall for the Bouwcentrum in Rotterdam. He had to design a "sculptured" surface of 62 × 28 feet and in brick, a material in which he had never worked before. This time it was not a matter of carving, but, according to the contract, of a demonstration of the potentialities of brickwork. Moore kept modestly in the background; nevertheless, the wall he designed goes far beyond the terms of his contract.

Had he any prototypes for a task of this kind? Not in Europe, but there were brick buildings with sculptural reliefs in ancient Babylon as, for example, in the temple of the Mother Goddess Innina at Warka dating from the middle of the second millennium, with serpents in relief and figures cut into the surface. There could be some connexion, but it is not very likely that Moore saw anything like it in one of the archaeological museums.

Again, he made several models; the second (Plate 140) bears an astonishing resemblance to the Islamic stucco ornaments in the Syrian monastery at Deir es-Surjani in Lower Egypt (AD 913), which were designed for conditions of profound darkness; there are also candelabra, crowns, pricked out triangles, squares and bosses in Moore's maquette. The fourth design with its bamboo lattices and the pattern of studs (Plate 141) is like the ornamental sections of the temple at Warka. The final maquette (Plate 142) returns to the horizontal of the 'Time and Life' screen, while retaining the bamboo lattices and the ornamentation.

Had Moore sought outside "stimuli", he would have been an eclectic. He is the reverse: he creates these shapes because the memory of ancient things is within him, he brings them up out of the depth of ancestral oblivion. If we none the less compare his work with historically demonstrable realities, this is to show how closely an artist of Moore's calibre is in harmony with the memories of mankind. "Tout l'univers visible n'est qu'un magasin d'images et de signes, auquel l'imagination donnera une place et une valeur relative," wrote Baudelaire.

Moore brings into being, invents, transforms and attains a result that casts off all the slag of experimentation and annuls all external stimuli, if there have been any. The result in this case is a wall divided up and covered with shapes typical of Henry Moore that reveal only a hint of their meaning. They are scarcely figures, certainly organic, growing, and they merge into the pattern of the brickwork as it rises course upon course.

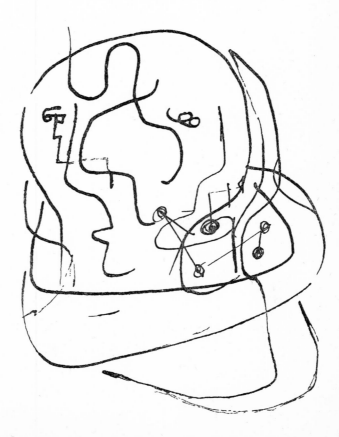

138

139

140

141

143

# STANDING FIGURES AND GLENKILN CROSSES

The 'Standing Figure', the chief theme of Greek classicism, did not come to interest Moore until very late. In the early years there were two, which he destroyed and threw away, and at the beginning of the 1930s two kneeling figures in wood, very close to standing ones, that he also abandoned. He began in 1950 with a 'Standing Figure' that seems straight away to exhaust all the composition's possibilities, just as, at the time when he began the series of 'Reclining Figures', he grasped all the opportunities offered by this composition in the "Mexican" figure of 1929.

The abstract 'Standing Figure' of 1950 (bronze, Plates 147, 148) which today, like the 'King and Queen' and the 'Glenkiln Cross', stands in the Scottish Highlands on the property of Mr W. T. Keswick, at Glenkiln, Dumfries, is a composition that does not surprise us, in view of the year in which it was produced. There are drawings for it dating from 1948. In 1950 came the 'Helmets', in 1951 the terrifying 'Reclining Figure' in the Musée d'Art Moderne in Paris.

The fact that the 'Rocking Chairs', those gay improvizations, also date from 1950 merely confirms again that Moore is not one of those sculptors who 'devour themselves' as one of his young English colleagues expressed it. He was thinking of the many sculptors for whom consistency and necessity are everything.

This monument—for that is what it looks like when seen in the Scottish landscape— Moore called a 'Standing Figure' which suggests that he is thinking of something organic, something human. Probably, however, he is thinking a great deal more of how something may grow out of a pair of supports and how out of this something else can grow, until a point comes at which he calls a halt, because these supports will never become articulated members if their succession remains unmotivated. They must be linked at intervals by horizontal shapes, so that even without association knee and pelvis are formed, and up above the shoulders. Shoulders? Perhaps, if they follow the structure and choose the shape of an acute-angled triangle. The head must then be double, according to the rules of the figure, for now it is already a figure, not a scaffolding. Thus on two necks there stand two heads, whose function as heads is clear to us from earlier compositions. The head of a piece of sculpture must not correspond to the spiritual and biological centre of gravity; it is rather the terminal accent of the composition. If it is double, as Moore had made this one, the open space that not only penetrates the figures, but plays around them like the clouds and the birds in the sky, endows it with the character of a gigantic group that confronts the landscape on equal terms.

The 'Standing Figure' is not demonic like the skeletal 'Reclining Figure' because, for one thing, it is sexless. To suppose that it is an angel, as E. Neumann believes ('The

Architypal World of Henry Moore', 1959), is not altogether far-fetched, when we think of the requiem with the many angels Klee made during the last year of his life The only difference is that Klee called up the angels, fashioned and named them; transcendency of form marched hand in hand with the transcendency of his imagery into the realm of the eschatological. Moore's situation is different; transcendency of form flows back into the figure and fills it with a multiplicity that belongs to the realm of the spiritual, but is not something outside existence.

The 'Standing Figure' held its place within the range of Moore's ideas. Between 1952 and 1955 he produced seven single figures and one group of three. The standing women of 1952 (all in bronze, Plates 151—153) vary greatly one from the other. The thin concave stature of the clothed figures recalls the Queen; the one with her arms raised above her head is a fully rounded version of the 'Standing Figure' in Scotland; the 'Leaf Figure' (Plate 153) is a bizarre version of the earlier degenerate women who are more like young girls.

The older Moore becomes, the greater the freedom and versatility of his inventiveness. He gets younger with age, turned more towards the world, which he is also better able to master; not only that part of the world, which moves him inwardly, but also what comes to him from outside. Now, a much travelled man, famous through his work, he occupies a place in public life, receives visitors from all over the world, and attains a more and more objective view of himself. Past fifty, he can look back over his achievement; perhaps he has already accomplished what he set out to do. The latest 'Standing Figures' are productions that have come into being effortlessly alongside big commissions and self-imposed tasks. Perhaps the 'Leaf Figures' are a game of his imagination for which, in his younger years, he was too serious. Is this creature we have never seen and never will see a masquerade or the entry into consciousness of a hitherto unused stratum? What does Moore mean by the 'Standing Figure' of 1955 (plaster for bronze, Plate 154)? It is vertical, eroded stone with hollows and holes and a neck which is at the same time a head. There is a hint of the human in a torso from which everything has been lopped off. After the decadence of 1952 (drawing, Plate 150, bronze, 1952, Plate 149). We have met the heads before, shapes worked by the human hand and then thrust back into the Old Stone Age. Nor can we turn to drawings for assistance during these years, for Moore does virtually no drawing at all. He employs this method of dealing with his subject only in very rare instances, for example in connection with the three 'Standing Figures' of 1952 (drawing, Plate 150, bronze 1952, Plate 149). We have met the heads before, in the three fateful figures from the period of the shelter drawings (1941) — only the heads, not the "African" bodies that carry the heads. They cannot be identified with the three goddesses of destiny in Battersea Park but they are their maleficent counterpart.

In the drawings for these figures, Moores leaves a great deal to the independent will of the line, which forms the trunk of the right-hand figure and repeats the triangle of the ruff in the hips. The joints are hinges, pure function but the shoulders are more like drapery. As a sculptor, Moore proceeds on different lines and probably began with the heads, for they determine the rest. These are sidereal heads, a half moon, a double star, a bird's head, mounted above the neck-rings and the shoulders. Are these skeletal structures or garments? It makes no difference whether the head on the right rises out of a shawl-collar or out of the cavern of the trunk, whether the two holes in the collar of the left-hand figure are breasts or part of the garment. Hips and knees interrupt the course of the verticals as in the 'Standing Figure' in Scotland with which they have a closer connexion than with the three prophetesses in Battersea Park. They also follow upon these works in time. These are deities of the underworld who do not seek the absolute, but the chthonic. That they appear "African" is probably due to their resemblance to house-posts in the Cameroons and arises particularly from the heads, which are exactly like the bronze sword handles that have existed in the Congo since time immemorial and are still to be found there today. These handles consist of half moons with a spike in the centre, or other, antenna-like shapes. This triad of Moore's is as old as time, but it could not be created until today. There is magic here too; it is not we who seek refuge with the figures, but they who seek refuge with us.

The 'Standing Figures' reach their culmination in the 'Upright Motives' of 1955 and 1957 (bronze, Plates 155—160). They are still almost unknown, and yet something like a legend has formed around them. They are sometimes known as 'Glenkiln crosses', although only one 'Upright Motive' takes this name from the owner's place of residence in Scotland, or as 'Scottish crosses', after the tall crosses in Scotland, Ireland and Wales dating from the early Middle Ages, although the one in Glenkiln is cruciform. In any case, the 'Upright Motives' have little more connexion with these Christian stones than with the Celtic menhirs or the ancient Assyrian obelisks in the British Museum. The sculptures began while Moore was designing the wall for the Bouwcentrum and extend over a good two years. He calls them 'Upright Motives', preferring as he does to avoid metaphorical titles, in order not to turn the attention of the observer from the object on to its associations. There are nine such 'Motives' of various sized in plaster, some of which have been cast in bronze.

The so-called 'Glenkiln Cross' (Plates 155, 156) is 9 feet tall and stands beside a loch in the Highlands, as if it had stood there through the ages and was not the work of human hands; or, if of human origin at all, then made so long ago it had been forgotten. The transverse member is as high up as in the Early Christian tau cross with a handle at the top which was originally a vital symbol, and the topmost member resembles the handle. The 'Glenkiln Cross' surely has more connexion with life than with death. A partially fluted shaft swells out into a bulge, from which rises an irregular column surmounted by the transverse member which fundamentally, is a spreading, organic shape and might just as well be a nesting eagle. There is something swelling about the whole upper half of this 'Motive' that is more animal than vegetal. The hallucinatory 'Animal Head' of 1951, or the 'Goat's Head' of 1952 are not more clearly related to the subject matter in their modelling than is the upper portion of the "cross". The observer wavers between animal and man, the sensual and the sublime, but the sublime in stronger—how else could the monument dominate the landscape? It dominates it in the way in which a Christian cross stands watch over a landscape. In the case of the Christian Cross people know its meaning; not in the case of the 'Glenkiln cross'. They feel it to be a local deity and hear the call of Pan, the god of flocks and shepherds, who could strike terror in men, but might also appear as a divine helper. The monument is a symbol of something that exists, not something that ought to exist, and is full of disturbing life.

There are monuments known to us in nature and art to which it seems almost pretion, even if in detail the shapes vary from the exuberant to the petrified. Bosses, studs and furrows appear, as in the brick wall in Rotterdam, and alongside them shapes that cling like shellfish or sea creatures to the rhythmically mobile shafts. The holes and grooves are meant to suggest weathering, the gristly formations, scar tissue; the emergence of human shapes in the 'Motive' with the crooked capital and the last one (Plates 159, 160) may be an optical illusion, but why should not man also put in an appearance among these baroque wonders?

There are monuments known to us in nature and art to which it seems almost preposterous to apply aesthetic standards. Does this make them something other than art, and what does art mean? In the course of our century much has come to be considered art that previously was not—the works of the primitive peoples, of the Cyclades, of the Nomadic tribes. Antiquity is not the criterion, but validity and unity of style and the fact that a new reality has been created which makes it possible to "view the invisible". The 'Upright Motives' are completely Moore and yet anonymous, universal and transcendental, sacred though not Christian, and they possess the same degree of absoluteness as all timeless art.

It is difficult to come to terms with the 'Upright Motives'. Everchanging, they look like tomb stelae at one moment, at another like totem poles, then achieve a poignancy, like something still agonizing over its own existence, or they may appear triumphant,

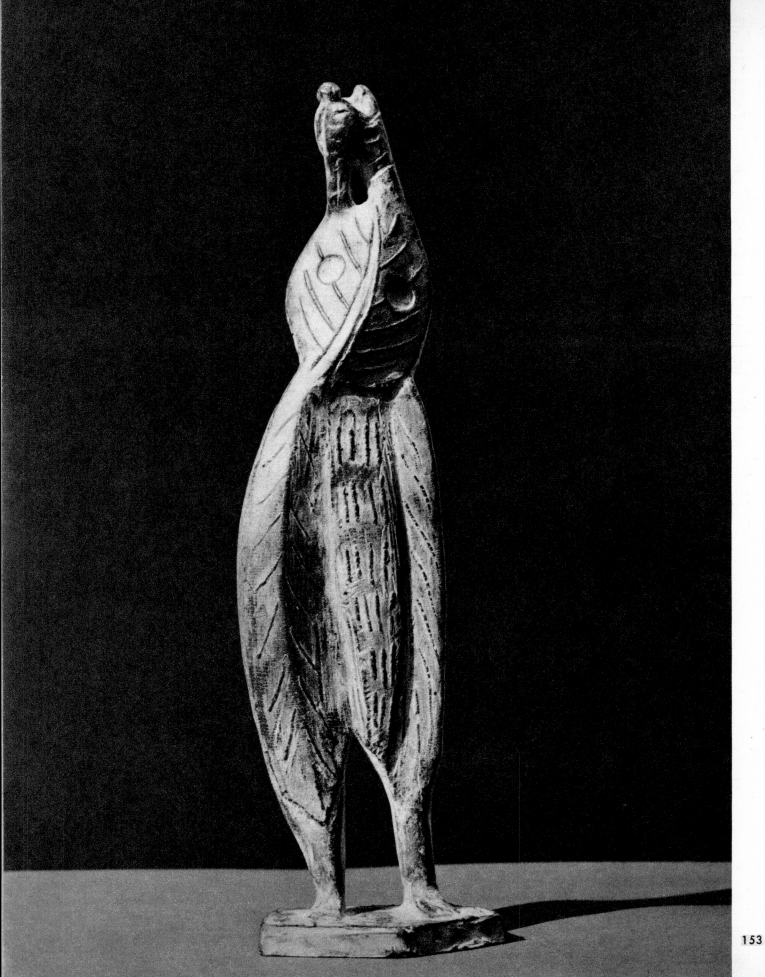

157

as though their life were already behind them and they were now resting in eternity. This fluctuation in one's reaction to these pieces is partially due to sudden shifts in which the organic suddenly breaks off and turns into matter and architectural elements such as columns and pillars take on a divine appearance and become spiritual expressions. Fragmentary sections of a column or of fluting, of a foot or a capital, in conjunction with hints of the corporeal, call up visions as bewildering as a grove of columns and stumps of columns at an excavation site. What place could be meant? Despite individual pointers to early epochs round the Mediterranean, the Celtic background of Moore's extraction comes to mind more readily. The style of Deir es-Surjani is the same as that of Celtic art with its zoomorphic and abstract forms, its riddles and interpenetrations. Characteristic of Moore's later years is that the Nordic element in his expression comes out more strongly and the Classical element, where it appears, plays a compensatory role. The style of the 20th century has been enriched by an important idiom through Moore's work.

remember
New Ireland
sculpture
for concrete
construction
experiments in
construction
* in concrete

# THE WARRIOR

The 1950s were full of harsh contrasts. Alongside the 'Greek' women stand terrifying figures like that of the mother with the vulture-like child, alongside the 'King and Queen' the mythological animal heads. The tension between his menacing mythico-tragic figures and the calm figures inspired by the Acropolis was stretched to break-ing-point in 1952 when Moore began the 'Warrior', a work that was to keep him busy longer than he could have anticipated.

Up to now, the man had never played a solo role in Moore's work. In the 'Family Groups' he is an equal among equals; in the 'King and Queen' he is scarcely felt as an antithesis to the queen, and in the series of lithographs from 'Prometheus' (Goethe, trans. Gide, 1950, colour plate page 237) he is anything but a son of the Titan, a rebel; he is more of an Epimetheus than a 'provider'. That Moore, the herald of motherhood and the chthonic deities of the underworld, should have come to create a 'Warrior', moreover such a severely mutilated one, and then go on to a 'Falling' and a 'Fallen Warrior' (1952-7, bronze, Plates 161—168), cannot be ex-plained by his war experience in London or the re-awakening of dreamlike memories of the First World War. It is certainly not the remoteness in time that makes this unlikely, but the figure of the 'Warrior' itself, which has nothing to do with the anonymous, technological mass slaughter. Taking Moore's mentality into account, it would be reasonable to see in him the break through of Dionysus into the gynaeco-cracy if he were not so devoid of sensuality. He is only a warrior, the prototype of the warrior, who has been defeated and mutilated in a murderous battle such as Homer sings of, who has lost his left arm and left leg and right foot, who has no weapon left but his shield, behind which he hides the remnant of his pitiable existence. A figure from the Mycenean epoch, his cloven head points to tragedy, the mouth is sewn together and mute, the eyes are holes.

The version without a shield is even more agonizing than that with the shield; the long right arm clutches senselessly in the void, whereas in the other version the shield supports the figure and the whole sculpture and gives it balance. The treatment of the surface is rough and cracked, as though to prevent a tautness and nobility of the physique from diminishing the tragedy of this Patroclus figure.

Most brutal of all are the 'Falling Warrior' and the 'Fallen Warrior', the latter with a slackly dangling left arm and a shield by the right foot, the former with stiffly supporting right arm and shield over the head. The 'Fallen Warrior' is the more helpless, the 'Falling Warrior' (the final version) has more dignity. In both, the move-ment of sprawling, falling, propping himself up and lying on his back is seen from all sides and, as we walk round the figure, the view changes with every step.

From some viewpoints the 'Fallen Warrior' looks like a miserable reptile, especially as the head is not much more than a perforated, elongated knob and the long arms and legs those of a lifeless puppet. There is nothing conciliatory about this fallen hero, nothing that mitigates the brutality, and perhaps that is why Moore modified him. The other version, the 'Falling Warrior', by contrast, is so apt and so rich in its details that in contemplating it, the observer's admiration for the sculptural achievement diverts his attention from the catastrophe. He remains caught up in the trance created by the combination of plastic and psychic values, by the discontinuity of the intersections, by the rhythm imparted to movements and breaks in movement.

This is how the chroniclers of the Trojan War saw heroes. The improbability and brutality of Moore's figure is beyond all topicality; the only contemporary element is the sculptor's language that competes with the language of the poem. Although there is nothing epic in the 'Falling Warrior', it contains the essence of the Homeric tale. Legend for legend, art for art, the arc spanning time is lost in the infinite, doing away in the presence of this figure with the distinction between ancient and modern times, between poetry and sculpture.

165

166

167

# THE 'SEATED FIGURE' AS A SUBJECT

The 'Seated', as opposed to the 'Reclining' or 'Standing Figure', first emerged as a theme in Moore's work in 1955. There had been earlier seated figures — a mother with a child among the shelter drawings and in the 'Family Groups'. Now, however, Moore isolated the theme and, since 1955, has produced a number of compositions which, like the 'Reclining Figures', are the expression of a particular sculptural and psychological content.

Repose as waiting and repose as the springboard for movement, sitting as an expression of composure, as in the case of the archaic Greek goddesses, and sitting as an expression of the moment before rising, jumping up, going into action — this is the human aspect. Like the 'Reclining Figure' outside the 'Time and Life' building, the relaxed figures tend toward the classical, the tense ones toward the demonic. But whereas the classical figures of that period have a touch of the Maidens from the Acropolis, of the Greek korai, the 'Seated Figures' belong to our own day and age; they are superior, modern beings, guardians of a university, a museum or a public square. The demonic figures, on the other hand, are continuations of the destroyed and destroying themes that followed the end of the 1930s and the beginning of the 1950s, except that this time the composition is not based on hollow forms and an open framework, but on fully three-dimensional shapes that have been subjected to distortions that exercise a shock effect.

The sculptural problem was to combine the body and its volume, its introverted closed-in mass and its extraverted gestures, in a rhythm that would weld them into a single whole. This is a difficult task. It is rendered easier when 'blockiness' is an essential characteristic of the composition, but this quality is abandoned.

The 'Woman Seated on Steps' (plaster model, 1956; bronze 1958, Plates 170, 171) sits very erect, gazing out from the topmost step into space, her arms lightly propped up, her legs placed very naturally to one side, her body clad from the neck to above the knee in a closefitting garment that reveals the shapes of the body. This is a full, broad-shouldered figure whose monumental simplicity of the modelling compensates for the smallness of the head. The second 'Seated Figure' (bronze, 1957/8, Plates 172—174) is regal in forms and posture and filled with a noble simplicity; she sits with her elongated head slightly bent, as though she had just woken up. Her garment is so adjusted that, in spite of all its folds, her body appears as distinctly as if she were unclothed. Everything flows, as though this woman had risen from moisture, as though she were an Anadyomene, born of the foam, the daughter of Zeus. The legend relates that during the mutilation of Uranus drops of his blood fell into the sea, and from them Anadyomene was conceived. We think of the mutilated 'Warrior' that precedes her, and feel inclined to let our imagination pursue the legend.

The treatment of the surfaces becomes more and more differentiated: the skin is porous; the folds of drapery are worked to give the greatest possible diversity; they are projecting and smooth, indented to the verge of perforation and then moulded in high relief. Different photographs create totally different impressions, depending on the way the light plays upon the surface. Moore does not calculate these effects in advance, however, but leaves it to the light to operate as it will. This enriches the rhythm of the interpenetrating members of the sculpture, a rhythm that is nowhere broken off and in the second 'Seated Figure' appears particularly impressively in the most laboriously modelled back view.

While working on the 'Reclining Figure' for the 'Time and Life' building in 1952, Moore found the contrast between figure and building stimulating. The idea of this combination continued to preoccupy him while he was working on the UNESCO commission, and from there he went on to experiment in this direction by creating the architecture himself, setting a seated woman in front of a curved wall, which he then placed at an angle, so that the space between it and the woman leaning forward opened out ('Draped Figure in front of a Wall', 1957, bronze, Plate 176). There are a few such compositions; the strange 'Dozing Figure' with the eloquent shadow on the wall (1957, bronze, Plate 175) falls under this heading. The 'Armless Figure', on the other hand, before a semicircular back-drop (1957, bronze, Plate 177) is as archaic and oracular as the ghostly, perforated giant leaf shape.

The demonic element is also still alive and emerges as the other aspect in the 'Seated Figures', no longer in an abstract shape, but corporeally and expressively. The 'Seated Figure' of 1955 (bronze, Plate 169) is closer to the divine than to the occult and menacing. The 1956 'Seated Girl', on the other hand, (Plates 183, 184), belongs to deeper regions, the hole in the chest, the cavern in her abdomen suggest an earthly origin; and finally the 'Seated Girl in front of a rectangular Wall' (1958, bronze, Plates 186, 187) leads into the darkest zones of human existence. It stands at the end of the path marked by certain preparatory works.

The 'Unclothed Seated Figure' of 1957 (bronze, Plates 179, 180) looks at first glance almost healthy and countryfied; but there is an unrest quivering in the sculptural emphasis of certain parts, the abdomen and left upper arm for example, that gives it an affinity with the 'Torso', the disproportionate female figure that one is most tempted to call Fate (bronze, 1957, Plates 181, 182). Fate not in the sense of the Battersea Park figures, but in the sense of the Roman goddess of birth, who retained her connexion with the powers of destiny. She is mutilated like the Warrior, but less wilfully and hence has "remained" a torso rather than "become" one. The arms are

230

missing and the legs stop at the knee, the chest is arched excessively far forward, the trunk swells out at the level of the inscribed navel, and the head sits small and timid on the tall neck, arousing a feeling of timidity in the observer. The whole composition is imbued with an aura of the superhuman and mysterious and is one of Moore's masterpieces.

The fragmentation of a piece of sculpture is not the sole factor that decides whether it is to be placed in the category of the demonic. As early as 1936, Moore produced a 'Seated Figure' (bronze, Plate 185) that is intact and yet, with its animal head, as terrifying as any ancient god.

The 'Seated Girl in front of a rectangular Wall' (Plates 186, 187) is a special case. An astonishingly "deformed" figure, with excessively long, thin legs, breasts displaced oddly upwards and an endlessly long neck topped by an elongated skull with eyes bored through it, she sits in front of a wall broken by horizontal and vertical set-backs that might be windows. This is a ghostly, surrealist situation in which figure and wall are on a par with one another, as are the organic and the inert, the mobile

Moore '51.

and the rigid, the spiritual and its enemy. The architectonic space is open and at the same time enclosed; the seated figure is free and at the same time imprisoned; but it is more of a dream world, removed from time and space, neither tragic nor terrible. The composition exists in an undefinable dream world and cannot be compared to anything.

## LATEST WORKS 1959

During recent months Moore has returned to the 'Mother and Child' with a bronze (1959, Plate 188) that breaks out of the framework established by its predecessors. The child is large and set erect on his mother's lap. The mother is open like a narrow gorge. Both are unarticulated and yet full of feeling. The more one looks at these two, the taller grows the child, and the more dominating and mysterious it becomes. It begins to seem like a devotional image with an erect Redeemer, as in Michelangelo's later 'Pietà' in Florence. The shapes change, but the relationship between man and eternity remains and demands expression in new and modern forms.

At the beginning of the year there came the bronze 'Three Motives against a Wall' (1928/9), a group of living beings that give the impression of being held in "statu nascendi", so much doubt surrounds their figures, in which the animal is combined with what is already human, the fragmented with what is not yet evolved and still amorphous. The composition seems to lead to the boundary of the possible and yet, if we compare it with the three 'Reliefs', of which two are finished and the third still in the process of being made (1959, plaster to be cast in bronze, Plates 190—192), it can be seen to be entirely within Moore's territory. These reliefs, huge works 7½ ft high, are figures of women that rise like menhirs or like towers on solid pillars. The modelling consists of deep cavities and projections and leaves no room for details. The second relief is more easily recognizable as a woman, but here too the masses rise and fall like strata and create a shape that bears only a faint resemblance to parts of the body. We must go back to prehistoric times in Egypt or South America to find comparable works. Only a few years ago one would not have believed Moore capable of bursting out of the framework of his previous achievement and thrusting on to productions involving not only figures of a new kind, but also a new approach to the processes of sculpture. The almost abstract reliefs are nature and art in one, and this must be the final synthesis.

Almost forty years have passed since Moore's first works, and he is still creating new compositions that give the world an answer drawn from the totality of his human existence. He has preserved his creative mobility and has never been afraid of abandoning a felicitous solution for the sake of a new one that is perhaps better or more complete. Success and fame have not overwhelmed him: the work, both in the process of working and its product, is more important than success.

He has revised many of his judgments and preconceived ideas, when he felt he had reached a truer insight, and has advanced step by step with the aid of complete inner honesty. The pattern that underlies his work, the formative energy that permeates everything, has remained the same; each of his carvings and models is a Moore and he has been fortified against influences of all kinds by his original attachment to nature and time. He is involved with the process of creation and he finds himself only where this process, and not ultimate perfection, reigns. For him, perfection in sculpture means to evolve the perfect idiom for each composition.

It is almost easier to see the unity in Moore's work than to understand his development. Although Moore has never failed to go his own way, it has been a way with detours. A sculptor who started in 1922 may have had more difficulties than an older man who started, say, in 1912. A great deal had already happened, the great breakthrough had already been achieved, anyone who followed had to take his place in the ranks or wait till he was given the password. But the talented receive the password from the world with its facts and questions. Since form is the organization of human experience, the artist is at all times faced with a difficult start; but it is doubly difficult when the pillars of spiritual and social life have crumbled, when the old categories of thinking and perceiving have proved invalid and the new are still in flux. It would seem that Moore put his trust in his own inner daemon; the attachment to his own self as the subject of his whole psyche, including its unconscious elements, was so decisive that initially the environment disturbed him little. The self stood over him like something suprapersonal and led him into the realm of Motherhood. Since a psychic constitution like Moore's is unalterable, his early works, all differences notwithstanding, show the same attitude as the late ones; what changes is the scope of experience and the degree of mastery over the vocabulary of forms. Moore has worked with unparalleled intensity for its extension and intensification.

The solid, central, three-dimensional and vital sculptures of the 1920s were followed by the surreal compositions of the 1930s, those enclosed within themselves like signs and the open ones, of which some advance outwardly to the boundaries of the technological, while others go to the limits of the demonic and on into the darkness of the earth. The 1940s, the war and post-war years, revealed to Moore precisely the sunny side of life in the shape of community and tradition, both religious and humanist so that the archaic and earthy retired into the background. But this was only a transitory stage, and the 1950s led Moore into situations where tension and relaxation reached their maximum. The "Greek" element is an incidental component; the absolute and the chthonic, on the other hand, show through everywhere and produce such contrasting works as the 'Standing Figures' and the mythological 'Cross' in Scotland, or the 'King and Queen' and the 'Warrior'. There is no fissure anywhere; everything comes from the same centre; only the manifestations vary.

Moore has been misunderstood in two directions and blamed on the one hand for his "naturalism" or "classicism", and on the other for his abstraction. But for Moore both were not a goal, but a path, and the leap to the one was no less bold than to the other. After so many experiments in the 1930s, to make a 'Madonna' or a 'Family Group' for a school playground demanded the same effort as to fashion a 'Reclining Figure' as the open repository of earthiness; a 'Reclining Figure' in the style of the Parthenon was just as hazardous an enterprise as the 'Outer and Inner Forms'.

It is not vacillation, but a process of self-testing, when Moore utilizes apparently opposed forms of expression; the pluralism of his consciousness is paralleled by a multiplicity of modes of expression, archaic and new. "The totality of all possible events is integrated in the limitless virtuality of our consciousness," says Paul Valéry. "It also combines the individual with the past of the species, with the world of symbols." The situation is the same in the works of Moore as in Joyce's 'Ulysses' or Stravinsky's 'Rite of Spring'. What seems contradictory in many of his works, the archaic expression and the technological framework, is in reality an expression of his capacity for working within many dimensions at the same time, which is one of the maturing sculptor's most remarkable characteristics. It gives his work the mysterious richness, the radiation that is as exciting as the world in which we live.

Eliot, as we recalled, stated that it is a man's sincerity that can be judged by his contemporaries. Part of this sincerity consists in having the courage to correct a mistake. For the first ten years, Moore saw the meaning of his work as a sculptor in 'blockiness' and volume and plasticity and the values connected with it; modelling in clay appeared to him a betrayal. He revised this opinion in the course of his development, not because the other view was brought to him from outside, but because he discovered the value of the open and dynamic in comparison with the closed and static, the expression of the absolute and demonic in comparison with the landscape-like and earthy. It must be established, however, that Moore does not give up the old in favour of something new; the absolute of the 'Standing Figures' in Scotland is present in another fashion in the Mexican 'Reclining Figure', and the demonic element in the Scottish 'Crosses' also partakes of the qualities of the landscape on a higher plane. The combination of antitheses is rooted in Moore's psychological structure, in which nature in the shape of the collective unconscious stands next to spirit, vitality next to law. It is spirit that intervenes and organizes, that turns a manual activity into an artistic one, that prevents the motherhood origins of life from becoming an obsession. It is spirit that drives the artist to the most daring experiments, without which the present would cease to be the present and a transition to the next stage.

The inexplicable is an unavoidable part of every artistic conception; it is a "factum sui generis", the very thing that art is all about. When Goethe had written his 'Fairy Tale' he was at first unable to say what it meant, and asked his friends to tell him. The public, Moore said in a speech at Venice in 1952, has no natural relationship to art and expects from it a confirmation of its notions of social, spiritual and artistic ideality, most of which amount in practice to a majority decision reached without any good grounds. Nothing is further from Moore's wishes than to provoke, but he defends his compositions and himself even when the composition is the fulfilment of a specific commission, and he believes that society can do no more than wait, the state no more than guarantee the artist's freedom. In return society and state have a share in the advancement of human consciousness brought about by the artist, which redounds to the advantage of all, or, as Herbert Read succinctly put it: "Our objective is not pleasure or it is pleasure only incidentally. We have discovered that art has a biological function, that the artist is the sensitive organ of an evolving consciousness —of man's progressive apprehension and understanding of his universe."

162a

Prometheus depart ⑥

169

170

172

175

176

181

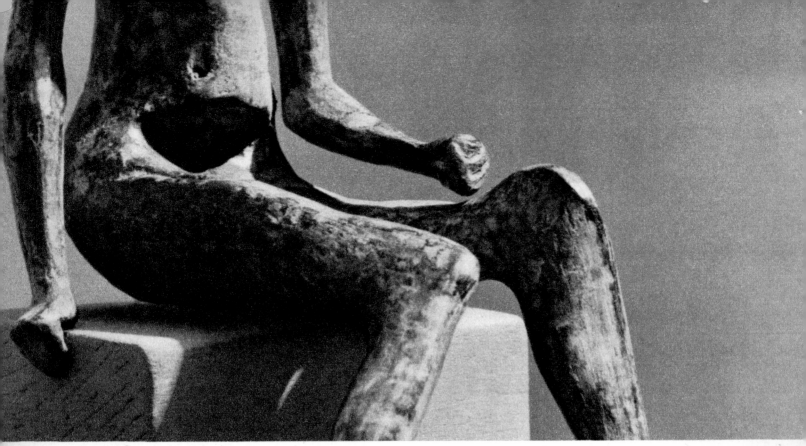

183

184

187

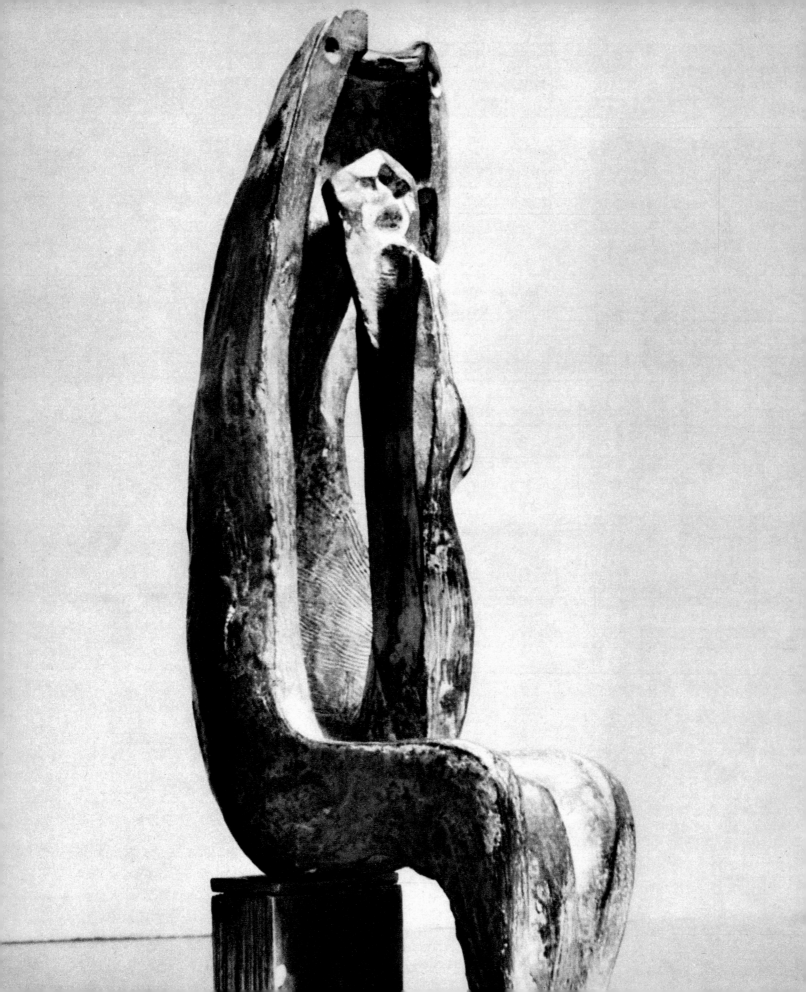

Henry Moore

# BIOGRAPHY

**1898** Born on 30th July in Castleford, Yorkshire, the seventh child of a miner, Raymond Spencer Moore and his wife, Mary, née Baker. Father of Irish descent.

**1910** Passes scholarship for grammar school. Encouraged by his art teacher, Miss Alice Gostik.

**1915** At his father's wish, becomes a teacher like three of the other Moore children.

**1916** Joins staff of his old elementary school in Castleford.

**1917** Joins army (Civil Service Rifles); goes to France in early summer, gassed in the Battle of Cambrai. Returns to hospital in England in December.

**1918** Promoted. Returns to France and army.

**1919** Demobilized in February. Returns to teaching a month later. In September obtains ex-servicemen's scholarship to the school of art at Leeds.

**1921** Wins sculpture scholarship to Royal College of Art, and so moves to London. Many visits to the British Museum. Interest in archaic and primitive sculpture.

**1922** Work in the open air during his holidays on the east coast.

**1923** First of his almost yearly visits to Paris.

**1925** Receives travelling-scholarship, but first concludes studies at Royal College and begins to teach there. Seven-year contract as teacher of sculpture.

**1926** After teaching for two months, spends six months abroad: Paris, Rome, Florence, Padua, Ravenna and Venice.

**1927** Exhibits for first time with other artists in the St George's Gallery, London.

**1928** First official commission for headquarters of London Transport. First one-man exhibition, in the Warren Gallery, London.

**1929** Marries Irina Radetsky, student at the Royal College of Art.

**1932** After the elapse of his contract with the Royal College, teaches twice weekly at the Chelsea School of Art.

**1933** Member of 'Unit One' a new English art-group.

**1934** Buys country house at Kingston near Canterbury.

**1936** Takes part in the International Surrealist Exhibition at the New Burlington Galleries. Visits Madrid, Toledo, Barcelona and the cave-paintings in the Pyrenees and Altamira.

**1939** Gives up teaching when the Chelsea School of Art is evacuated, and moves to Kingston.

**1940** Returns to his London studio in August. 'War artist' until 1942. Begins the shelter drawings. After partial destruction of London studio, moves to Much Hadham, Hertfordshire, where he still lives with his family.

**1941** Appointed a Trustee of the Tate Gallery for seven years, reappointed in 1949.

**1945** Honorary doctorate of Leeds University. Visit to Paris in November for the first time since the war.

**1946** Birth of a daughter, Mary. Visit to New York on the occasion of his first big retrospective exhibition, held in the Museum of Modern Art.

Moore's Mother,

Moore's Father, 1871.

1948 Honoured at home and abroad. Receives international sculpture prize at 24th Venice Biennale. Visits Florence, Pisa, Venice.

1949 Visits Brussels, Amsterdam, Berne.

1951 Corresponding member of the Swedish Royal Academy of Fine Arts. Visit to Greece (Athens, Mycene, Olympia, Corinth, Delphi).

1952 Takes part in one of the congresses of international artists arranged by UNESCO in Venice. Visits Florence and Rome.

1953 Honorary doctorate of letters from London University. International sculpture prize in second São Paolo Biennale. Visit to Brazil and Mexico.

1954 Visits Milan, Venice, Rome, Rotterdam, Hanover.

1955 Trustee of National Gallery, London. Visits to Yugoslavia, the Rhineland and Holland.

1956 Again in Holland.

1957 Awarded the Stephan Lochner medal by the city of Cologne. Goes to Italy to sculpt the UNESCO figure in the marble quarries of Querceta.

1958 Visits America. Honorary doctorate of fine arts from Harvard University. Visits New York and San Francisco. Later, journey to Poland. Awarded sculpture prize by the Carnegie Institute, Pittsburgh, USA.

1959 Honorary doctorate of law from Cambridge University. Awarded international sculpture prize in Tokyo.

Henry Moore when a Soldier. 1917.

The House in which Moore was born.

His Marriage. 1929.

Henry Moore in 1930 with his Wife Irina.

With his Daughter Mary, 1951.

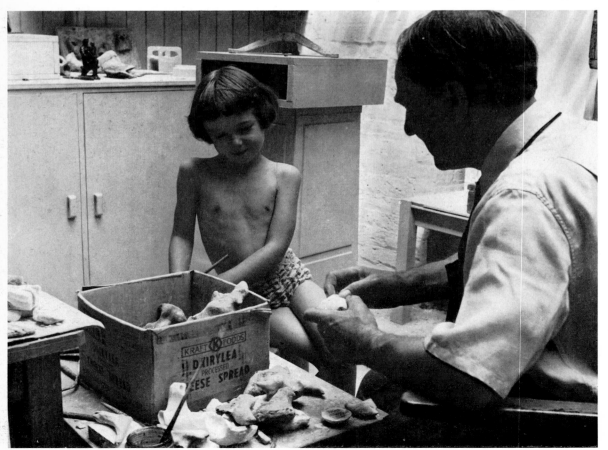

Venice. 1954.

Stonehenge. 1953.

In the Marble Quarries cf Querceta, choosing a Block for the UNESCO Figure.

*. I feel the conflict still exists in me — but not causing me any difficulty in working, as it did immediately after returning from Italy, — in fact I ask myself is this conflict what makes things happen? For it seems to me now that this conflict between the excitement & great impression I got from Mexican sculpture A, & the love & sympathy I felt for Italian art, represents two opposing sides in me, the "tough" & the "tender", & that many other artists have had the same two conflicting sides in their natures... Blake for example was torn between the two — his tender 'Songs of Innocence' & lyrical watercolours — & his tough muscular 'Nebuchadnezzar eating grass'. Goya could paint beautifully tender portraits of children, & yet painted the violent 'Satan devouring a child" (on his own dining-room wall!) Shakespeare wrote 'Romeo & Juliet' & 'Macbeth' & 'King Lear' (But we easily accept double sympathies in literature — & realize that Shakespeare's tragic & violent side was all the richer & deeper because he had the tender side!) Michaelangelo's art shows conflict — the bombastic ~~tough~~ insensitive ~~muscular~~ swagger of his 'David', & the slow lazy melancholy of 'Night' & 'Day'. Only at the end of a long life, in his greatest & last works are these qualities ~~mixed~~ to become a noble rich-blooded maturity of strength mingled with melancholy. &

And as I've suggested, what conflicting attitudes don't we find in the work of today's greatest painter, Picasso — (in ~~with~~ his so-called 'sweet & sentimental' blue period, (& his Greek vase loveliness) — of the violent recent work.) P

And really I see no difficulty in appreciating both sides & finding them in the same artist.

Perhaps a̶n̶ obvious & continuous synthesis will eventually derive in my own work — I can't say — I can only work as I feel & believe at the time I do the work.

1959.  Receives an Honorary Doctorate from Cambridge
(in front, Le Corbusier, behind him to the right, Moore).

An Exhibition in the Buchholz Gallery New York. 1951. (Curt Valentin)

Rome 1954 with Marino Marini (centre) and E. C. Gregory (right).

H. R. Fischer, Henry Moore, Will Grohmann. 1951.

The House at Much
Hadham with the
Sculptor at work on
the Time and Life
Screen. 1952.

His New Studio. 1959.

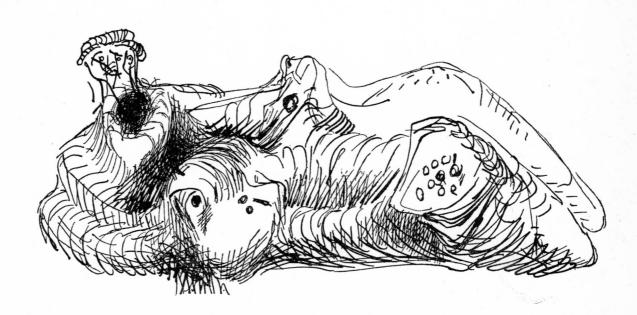

# BIBLIOGRAPHY

The bibliography contains only the most important publications on Henry Moore; if articles in periodicals are included, they already run into hundreds.

The author owes special thanks to Herbert Read and David Sylvester for their research on Moore, and to the psychologist Erich Neumann (see bibliography).

## Writings by Henry Moore

1 Statement in Architectural Association Journal, London, Vol. XLV, No. 519, May 1930, pp. 408—13, illus.

2 Statement in Unit One: The Modern Movement in English Architecture, Painting and Sculpture, Ed. Herbert Read, London, Cassell, 1934, pp. 27—35, illus.

3 'Mesopotamian Art'. The Listener, London, Vol. XIII, No. 334, June 1935, pp. 944—6, illus.

4 Quotations in Circle, an International Survey of Constructive Art, London, Faber & Faber, 1937, p. 118, illus.

5 'The Sculptor Speaks'. The Listener, London, Vol. XVIII, No. 449, August 1937, pp. 338—40, illus.

6 'Primitive Art'. The Listener, London, Vol. XXV, No. 641, April 1941, pp. 598—9.

7 'The Living Image: Art and Life' (discussion). The Listener, London, Vol. XXVI, No. 670, November 1941, pp. 657—9, illus.

8 'Note on the Madonna and Child Statue'. Transformation, London, No. 3, 1945, pp. 132—3, illus.

9 'Was der Bildhauer anstrebt'. Thema, Munich, Nr. 5, 1949, pp. 40—1, illus.

10 'Message de la Sculpture'. XXe Siècle, Paris (n. s.), No. 1, 1951, pp. 59—70, illus.

11 'Tribal Sculpture'. Man, Vol. LI, July 1951, pp. 95—6.

12 'Témoignage: L'Espace'. XXe Siècle, Paris (n. s.), No. 2, Jan. 1952, pp. 74—8, illus.

13 Interview with Ark Magazine. Ark, London, No. 6, Nov. 1952, pp. 10—3, illus.

14 'The Sculptor in Modern Society'. Art News, New York, Vol. V, No. 6, Nov. 1952, pp. 24—5, 64—5, illus. Also published in The Artist in Contemporary Society, an International Congress of Artists, Venice, 22—28 September 1952; Paris, Unesco, 1954, pp. 100—6.

15 'Notes on Sculpture'. The Creative Process. Ed. Ghiselin, Brewster, Berkeley and Los Angeles, University of California Press, 1952, pp. 68—73.

16 Statement in Art, Dec. 1953, pp. 9/10.

17 Extract from Letter to Canon Hussey, Northampton. The Country Churchman, May 1954, No. 2, No. 5, p. 3.

18 'The Hidden Struggle'. The Observer, 24. Nov. 1957. Extract from a book Conversations with Henry Moore by J. P. Hodin (in preparation).

## Books, Articles and Catalogues

AMSTERDAM, STEDELIJK MUSEUM. Henry Moore ... georganiseerd door The British Council, Amsterdam, 1950, 15 pp., illus, 97 works. Statement by Henry Moore, Foreword by Herbert Read.

ARGAN, GIULIO CARLO. Henry Moore, Torino, De Silva, 1948, 26 pp., 32 plates, portrait.

ARTS COUNCIL OF GREAT BRITAIN. A Retrospective Exhibition of Drawings by Henry Moore, London, 1948, 4-p. Intro. by A. D. B. Sylvester.

Do. Sculpture and Drawings by Henry Moore ... at the Tate Gallery, London, 1951, 20 pp., 44 plates. Catalogue by A. D. B. Sylvester.

BRITISH COUNCIL, London. Exhibition of Sculpture and Drawings by Henry Moore to be shown at the State Galleries of Sydney, Hobart, Melbourne, Adelaide, Perth; Melbourne, 1947, 23 pp. illus. Foreword by Clive Turnbull.

Do. Sculpture and Drawings by Henry Moore, Venice, Biennale 1948, London, Lund Humphries, 1948, illus. Intro. by Herbert Read, 69 works. Text and Catalogue published in Italian in the Catalogue of the XXIV Biennale di Venezia, 1948, pp. 275—281, illus.

BERN, KUNSTHALLE. Henry Moore, veranstaltet vom British Council und der Kunsthalle, Bern. Intro. by Herbert Read, Statement by Moore, 126 works, 6 photographs, 1950.

BUCHHOLZ GALLERY, CURT VALENTIN, New York. Henry Moore, 40 Watercolours and Drawings, New York, 1943. Catalogue contains 'Henry Moore, a Note on his Drawings' by Sir Kenneth Clark.

Do. The Drawings of Henry Moore, New York, 1946, 4 pp., 30 plates.

Do. Henry Moore, 32 Works and Drawings, Pastels, Watercolours, New York, 1954. Text by H. Moore: 'King and Queen' and 'Notes on Sculpture'.

CLARK, KENNETH. 'A Madonna by Henry Moore', Magazine of Art, Vol. XXXVII, Washington, D. C., Nov. 1944, pp. 247—9, illus.

COOPER, DOUGLAS. (Review of) 'Sculpture and Drawings', Horizon, Vol. X, No. 60, London, Dec. 1944, pp. 425—8.

FLEMMING, HANS THEODOR. Henry Moore: Karakomben, Munich, Piper, 1956, 16 pp., 45 plates.

FRANKFURT, MANNHEIM, MUNICH, STUTTGART, BERLIN, BREMEN, GÖTTINGEN. Henry Moore: Ausstellung von Plastiken und Zeichnungen, veranstaltet vom British Council, 1953, 6 pp. with biographical notes, Intro. by Herbert Read, Statement by Moore, illus., 2-col. plates.

HANOVER, KESTNER-GESELLSCHAFT. Henry Moore, 1953, 16 pp., illus., Foreword by Alfred Hentzen.

HEADS, FIGURES AND IDEAS. Sculptor's sketch book, lithograph frontispiece by Henry Moore. London, George Rainbird, 1958; New York, Graphic Society, 1958.

HENDY, PHILIP. 'Henry Moore', Horizon, Vol. IV, No. 21, London, Sept. 1941, pp. 200—6, illus.

Do. 'Humanists and Wild Ones', New Statesman, Vol. LVI, No. 1448, Dec. 1958, p. 853.

HODIN, J. P. Henry Moore, Amsterdam, Lange, 1956, 18 pp., 32 plates.

Do. 'Neuere Werke Henry Moores', Werk, Nr. 8, Zürich, August 1958, pp. 290—6, illus.

HOFMANN, WERNER. Ed. and Intro. to Henry Moore. Schriften und Skulpturen, Frankfurt a. M., Fischer Bücherei Nr. 250, 1959, 104 pp., 64 plates.

HUSSEY, REV. J. W. A. Statue of Madonna and Child in St Matthew's Church, Northampton, Northampton, 1945, 2 pp.

LEICESTER GALLERIES, LONDON. Catalogue of an Exhibition of Sculpture and Drawings by Henry Moore, London, 1931, 11 pp., 53 works, Foreword by Jacob Epstein.

Do. Bronzes and Drawings, London, 1951, 16 pp., illus., 57 works.

Do. New Bronzes, London, 1954, 16 pp., illus., 33 works.
MELVILLE, ROBERT. 'Henry Moore and the Siting of Public Sculpture', Architectural Review, Vol. CXV, London, Feb. 1954, pp. 87—95.

MIDDLETON, MICHAEL. 'Henry Moore', The Selective Eye, London, Zwemmer, 1955, pp. 162—9, illus. First published in French translation in L'Oeil, No. 3, Paris, March 1955, pp. 5—11. illus.

NEUMANN, ERICH. The Archetypal World of Henry Moore, New York, 1959, Bollingen Series LXVIII, Pantheon, 130 pp., illus.

ONSLOW-FORD, GORDON. 'The Wooden Giantess of Henry Moore', London Bulletin, No. 18—20, London, June 1940, p. 10, illus.

PARIS, MUSEE NATIONAL D'ART MODERNE. Henry Moore, organisée par le British Council, Paris, 1949, 12 pp., illus., 97 works Quotations from Moore, Intro. by Herbert Read.

PEVSNER, NIKOLAUS. 'Thoughts on Henry Moore', Burlington Magazine, Vol. LXXXVI, London, Feb. 1945, pp. 47—9.

RAMSDEN, E. H. 'Der Bildhauer Henry Moore', Werk, Vol. XXXIV, No. 4, Zürich, April 1947, pp. 129—35, illus.

## Book and Periodical Illustrations by Henry Moore

Contemporary Poetry and Prose, No. 9, London, Spring 1937. Cover drawing.

MOORE, HENRY. Shelter Sketch Book, London, Editions Poetry London, 1944; New York, Wittenborn, 1945; 2 pages and 82 plates. The drawings are taken from two original sketch books.

Poetry, Vol. II, No. 7, London, October-November 1942; No. 8, November-December 1942; Vol. III, No. 11, September-October 1947.

SACKVILLE-WEST, EDWARD. The Rescue, a Melodrama for Broadcasting based on Homer's Odyssey with six illustrations of the text by Henry Moore, London, Secker & Warburg, 1945, 96 pp. and 6 plates.

Do. Sculpture: Theme and Variations, London, Lund Humphries, 1953, 56 pp., illus.

READ, HERBERT. Henry Moore, Sculptor, London, Zwemmer, 1934, 16 pp., 36 plates.

Do. Henry Moore, Sculpture and Drawings, London, Lund Humphries; New York, Curt Valentin, 1944; 2nd Ed. 1946; 3rd Ed. revised and enlarged 1949; 4th Ed. completely revised 1957. Contains Statements and Essays by Moore, text by Herbert Read, edited by A. D. B. Sylvester.

Do. Henry Moore. Volume Two: Sculpture and Drawings since 1948, London, Lund Humphries; New York, 1955; 24 pp., 140 plates. Contains new contributions by Moore, edited by A. D. B. Sylvester. (These two volumes contain reproductions of almost all the works and complete documentation.)

STOKES, ADRIAN. 'Mr Henry Moore's Sculpture', The Spectator, Vol. CLI, London, Nov. 1933, p. 661.

STRACHAN, W. J. 'Henry Moore's Prométhée, Experiments for a book', Image, No. 8, London, Summer 1952, pp. 3—16, illus.

SUTTON, DENYS. 'Henry Moore and the English Tradition', Kingdom Come, Vol. II, No. 2, Oxford, Winter 1940/1, pp. 48—9.

SWEENEY, JAMES JOHNSON. Henry Moore, New York, Museum of Modern Art, 1946, 95 pp., illus.

SYLVESTER, A. D. B. 'Henry Moore: The Shelter Drawings', Graphis, Vol. II, No. 14, Zürich, March-April 1946, pp. 126—35, 262—3, illus. Text in English, French, German.

Do. 'Evolution of Henry Moore's Sculpture', Burlington Magazine, Vol. XC, London, June-July 1948, pp. 158—65, 189—95, illus.

SCHIMANSKI, STEFAN & TREECE, HENRY, ed. A Map of Hearts, London, Lindsay Drummond, 1944. Design for dust jacket.

GANYMEDE PRINTS OF SCULPTORS' DRAWINGS, London, Lund Humphries, 1950. Contains a colour reproduction by Henry Moore.

GOETHE, JOHANN WOLFGANG VON. Prométhée. Traduction par André Gide, Lithographies de Henry Moore, Paris, Henri Jonquières & P. A. Nicaise, 1950. Limited edition: 183 copies, 8 colour-lithographs.

HAWKES, JACQUETTA. A Land, with Drawings by Henry Moore, London, Cresset Press, 1951, 18 coloured drawings.

LEY, MURRAY HICKEY. A is All, San Francisco, Grabhorn Press, 1953, frontispiece and inside of dust jacket.

MOORE, HENRY. Original lithograph, XXe Siècle (n. s.), No. 1, Paris, 1951, facing p. 69.

## ONE-MAN EXHIBITIONS

1928 London. Warren Gallery. 93 works.

1931 London. Leicester Galleries. 34 sculptures and 19 drawings.

1933 London. Leicester Galleries. 19 sculptures and 20 drawings.

1935 London. Zwemmer Gallery. 45 drawings.

1936 London. Leicester Galleries. 19 sculptures and 16 drawings.

1939 London. Mayor Gallery. 31 drawings.

1940 London. Leicester Galleries. 20 sculptures and 31 drawings.

1941 Leeds. Temple Newsam. 36 sculptures and 59 drawings.

1943 New York. Buchholz Gallery. 40 drawings.

1945 London. Berkeley Galleries. 13 sculptures and 22 drawings.

1946 London. Leicester Galleries. 9 sculptures and 64 drawings.
     Washington. Phillips Memorial Gallery. Drawings.
     New York. Museum of Modern Art. 58 sculptures and 48 drawings.

1947 Chicago. Art Institute of Chicago. 58 sculptures and 48 drawings.
     San Francisco. Museum of Modern Art. 58 sculptures and 48 drawings.
     Sydney. National Gallery of New South Wales. 15 sculptures and 27 drawings.
     Hobart. Tasmanian Museum and Art Gallery. 15 sculptures and 27 drawings.
     Melbourne. National Gallery of Victoria. 15 sculptures and 27 drawings.
     Adelaide. National Gallery of Western Australia. 15 sculptures and 27 drawings.
     Perth. National Gallery of Western Australia. 15 sculptures and 27 drawings.

1948 Cambridge. Arts Council. 30 drawings.
     Venice. British Pavilion, 24 Biennale. 36 sculptures and 33 drawings.
     Milan. Galleria d'Arte Moderna. 36 sculptures and 33 drawings.
     London. Rowland Browse and Delbanco. 47 drawings and 17 models.

1949 Wakefield. City Art Gallery. 53 sculptures and 73 drawings.
     Manchester. City Art Gallery. 53 sculptures and 73 drawings.
     Brussels. Palais des Beaux Arts. 53 sculptures and 44 drawings.
     Paris. Musée National d'Art Moderne. 53 sculptures and 44 drawings.

1950 Amsterdam. Stedelijk Museum. 53 sculptures and 44 drawings.
     Hamburg. Kunsthalle. 53 sculptures and 44 drawings.
     Düsseldorf. Städtische Kunstsammlungen. 53 sculptures and 44 drawings.
     Bern. Kunsthalle. 53 sculptures and 44 drawings.
     Mexico City. Galeria de Arte Mexicano. 34 drawings.
     Guadalajara. 34 drawings.

1951 Athens. Zappeion Gallery. 53 sculptures and 44 drawings.
     London. Tate Gallery. 73 sculptures and 96 drawings.
     London. Leicester Galleries. 17 sculptures and 40 drawings.
     Berlin. Haus am Waldsee. 10 sculptures and 67 drawings.
     New York. Buchholz Gallery. 34 sculptures and 31 drawings.
     Vienna. Albertina. Drawings.

1952 Cape Town. National Gallery of South Africa. (Van Riebeeck Tercentenary Celebrations.) 23 sculptures and 36 drawings.
     Stockholm. Akademien. 23 sculptures and 30 drawings.
     Norrköping. Akademien. 23 sculptures and 30 drawings.
     Orebro. Akademien. 23 sculptures and 30 drawings.
     Göteborg. Kunstmuseum. 23 sculptures and 30 drawings.
     Linz. Neue Galerie der Stadt Linz. 31 drawings and 10 small bronzes.
     Stockholm. Samlaren Gallery. 24 sculptures and 16 drawings.

1953 Copenhagen. Kunstforeningen. 23 sculptures and 30 drawings.
     Oslo. Kunstnernes Hus. 23 sculptures and 30 drawings.
     Trondheim. Kunstforeningen. 23 sculptures and 30 drawings.
     Bergen. Kunstforeningen. 23 sculptures and 30 drawings.
     Rotterdam. Boymans Museum. 28 sculptures and 43 drawings.
     London. Institute of Contemporary Arts. 106 drawings.
     Antwerp. Comite voor Artistieke Werking. 15 sculptures and 24 drawings.
     Hanover. Kestner-Gesellschaft. 24 sculptures and 38 drawings.
     Munich. Haus der Kunst. 24 sculptures and 38 drawings.
     Frankfurt. Staedelsches Kunstinstitut. 24 sculptures and 38 drawings.
     Stuttgart. Staatsgalerie. 24 sculptures and 38 drawings.
     São Paulo. British Section, 2nd International Biennial of São Paulo. 29 sculptures and 40 drawings.

1954 London. Leicester Galleries. 33 sculptures.
Mannheim. Kunsthalle. 24 sculptures and 38 drawings.
Bremen. Kunsthalle. 24 sculptures and 38 drawings.
Berlin. Schloss Charlottenburg. 24 sculptures and 38 drawings.
Göttingen. Stadtverwaltung. 25 sculptures and 38 drawings.
New York. Curt Valentin Gallery. 32 sculptures and 20 drawings.

1955 Basel. Kunsthalle. 39 sculptures and 55 drawings.
Boulder. University of Colorado. 50 drawings.
Colorado. Colorado Springs Fine Arts Centre. 50 drawings.
Denver. Denver Art Museum. 50 drawings.
Wyoming. University of Wyoming. 50 drawings.
Zagreb. 27 sculptures and 24 drawings.
Belgrade. 27 sculptures and 24 drawings.
London. Leicester Galleries. 22 sculptures and 17 drawings.
Ljubljana. 27 sculptures and 24 drawings.
Montreal. Museum of Fine Arts. 35 sculptures and 32 drawings.
Ottawa. National Gallery of Canada. 35 sculptures and 32 drawings.

1956 Toronto. The Art Gallery. 35 sculptures and 32 drawings.
Winnipeg. The Art Gallery Ass. 35 sculptures and 32 drawings.
Vancouver. The Art Gallery. 35 sculptures and 32 drawings.
Auckland. City Art Gallery. 35 sculptures and 32 drawings.
Dunedin. Public Art Gallery. 35 sculptures and 32 drawings.
Christchurch. Canterbury Soc. of Arts. 35 sculptures and 32 drawings.

1957 Paris. Galerie Berggruen. 30 sculptures and 32 drawings.
Wellington. National Art Gallery of New Zealand. 35 sculptures and 32 drawings.
Port Elizabeth, New Zealand. King George VI Art Gallery. 35 sculptures and 32 drawings.
Salisbury. Rhodes National Gallery. 35 sculptures and 32 drawings.
Bulawayo. National Museum. 35 sculptures and 32 drawings.

1958 Johannesburg. Art Gallery. 35 sculptures and 32 drawings.
Holland. Sonsbeek '58. 19 sculptures.
Newcastle-upon-Tyne. Hatton Gallery. 38 sculptures.
London. Marlborough Fine Art Ltd. 4 sculptures.

1959 Lisbon. Palacio Foz.
Oporto. Escola de Bellas Artes.
Madrid. Galleries of the National Library Building.
Barcelona. Santa Cruz Hospital.
London. Marlborough Fine Art Ltd.
Tokyo. Metropolitan Art Gallery.
Osaka. Sogo Department Store.
Takamatsu. Art Gallery of Takamatsu City.
Yawata. Art Gallery of Yawata City.
Hiroshima. Fukuya Department Store.
Fukuoka. Daimaru Department Store.
Ube. City Hall.
Saseho.
Nakamura. Nakamura Department Store.
Antwerp. Middelheim Park. 15 sculptures.
Warsaw. Zachenta Gallery.
Cracow. Art Society.
Wroclaw. Central Committee for Art Exhibitions.

1960 Posen. National Museum.
Stettin. Museum.
Hamburg. Kunsthalle. Thirty Years of Henry Moore.
Essen. Folkwang-Museum. Thirty Years of Henry Moore.
Zürich. Kunsthaus. Thirty Years of Henry Moore.
Munich. Haus der Kunst. Thirty Years of Henry Moore.

## MUSEUMS AND PUBLIC COLLECTIONS POSSESSING SCULPTURES BY HENRY MOORE

Aberdeen Art Gallery, Scotland.
Adelaide Gallery, Australia.
Amsterdam, Stedelijk Museum.
Atlanta Art Museum, USA.
Baltimore Museum, USA.
Basle, Kunstmuseum.
Berlin, Galerie des 20. Jahrhunderts.
Birmingham, City Museum and Art Gallery.
Bloomfield Hills, Michigan, Cranbrook Academy of Art.
Boston, Museum of Fine Arts.
Brussels, Musées Royaux des Beaux Arts.
Buffalo, Albright Art Gallery.
Chicago, Art Institute of Chicago.
Dorset, Poole College, England.
Freiburg i. Brsg., Universität.
Hanover, Niedersächsische Landesgalerie.
Harvard University, Fogg Art Museum.
Iowa, Blanden Memorial Gallery.
Eire, Friends of the National Collections of Eire.
Cologne, Stadt.
Leeds, City Art Gallery and Temple Newsam House.
London, Arts Council of Great Britain.
London, British Council.
London, Contemporary Art Society.
London, Tate Gallery.
London, Victoria and Albert Museum.
Manchester, City Art Gallery (Rutherston Loan Collection).

Mannheim, Städtische Kunsthalle.
Melbourne, National Gallery of Australia.
Mexico City, El Eco, The Experimental Museum of Mexico City.
Minneapolis Institute of Arts, USA.
Montreal, Fine Art Museum.
Munich, Staatliche Bayerische Kunstsammlungen.
Munich, Städtische Galerie.
New Haven, Yale University Art Gallery.
New York, Museum of Modern Art.
New York, Syracuse University.
Northampton, Mass., Smith College Museum of Art.
Oslo, Kunsternes Hus.
Ottawa, National Gallery of Canada.
Oxford, Worcester College.
Paris, Musée National d'Art Moderne.
Pittsburgh, Carnegie Institute.
Rio de Janeiro, Museu de Arte Moderna.
St Louis, City Art Museum.
St Louis, Washington University.
Toledo, Museum.
Tel Aviv, Museum.
Toronto, Art Gallery of Toronto.
Wakefield, City Art Gallery and Museum.
Washington, D. C., Phillips Memorial Gallery.
Wuppertal, Stadt. Zollikon-Zürich.
Zürich, Kunsthaus.

## PUBLIC COMMISSIONS

1928   North Wind. 96" long. Headquarters of the London Underground Railway.

1943/44   Madonna and Child. 59" high. Church of St Matthew, Northampton.

1945/46   Memorial. 56" long. Dartington Hall, South Devon.

1945/49   Family Group. 60" high. Barclay School, Stevenage.

1947/48   Three Standing Figures. 85" high. For the Contemporary Art Society; stands in Battersea Park, London.

1949   Madonna and Child. 48" high. Claydon Church, Suffolk.

1950/51   Reclining Figure. 51½" long. Erected in Temple Newsam, London.

1952/53   Screening Wall. 122" high × 323" long. — Draped Reclining Figure. 63" long. Time and Life Building, Bond Street, London.

1955   Brick Wall. 341½ high × 768" long. Bouwcentrum, Rotterdam, Holland.

1955   Family Group. 64" high. Harlow New Town, England.

1957/58   Reclining Figure. 200" long. UNESCO Building, Paris.

## ACKNOWLEDGEMENTS

Bo Boustedt 179, 180. Alfred Carlebach 108. Cracknell 82. Catherine Ducros 136. Gnilka 172, 174, 181, 182, dust wrapper. John Hedgecoe 21, 61, 62. Illustrated p. 268 below. Keystone p. 272 below. Lidbrooke 15, 33, 47, 48, 57, 63, 83, 93, 98, 99, 103, 118, 119, 141, 142, 154, 156, 158, 160, 162, 167, 169, 176, 177, 183, 184, p. 265. Felix H. Man 157. James Mortimer 14, 16, 28, 104. Simon Reid 134, 155. Barnet Saidman p. 272 above. Brian Seed 137. Adolf Studly 46, 81. The Times p. 271 above left. John Underwood 53. All other photographs by the artist.